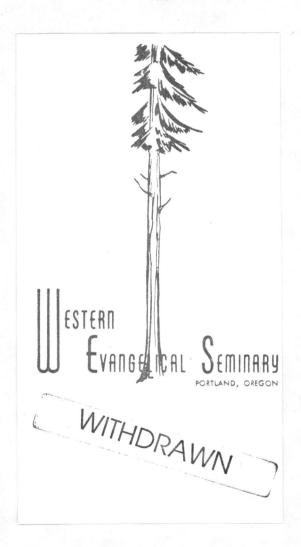

W ESTERN

E VANGELICAL S EMINARY

PORTLAND, OREGON

The Human Side of Enterprise

DOUGLAS McGREGOR

School of Industrial Management
Massachusetts Institute of Technology

McGRAW-HILL BOOK COMPANY, INC.

New York   Toronto   London   1960

THE HUMAN SIDE OF ENTERPRISE

TO MY WIFE

PREFACE

Some years ago during a meeting of the Advisory Committee of MITs School of Industrial Management, Alfred Sloan raised some questions related to the issue of whether successful managers are born or made. I was aware—as he was—that his questions were not easily answered. The discussion, however, served to sharpen certain interests I had had for some time in a systematic examination of the many common but inconsistent assumptions about what makes a manager.

In 1954 the Alfred P. Sloan Foundation made a grant to Alex Bavelas and me to explore some of these ideas more fully. Bavelas' interests lay in some laboratory experiments, while mine centered on research in industry, but they had a common focus on a more adequate theory of management.

After Bavelas went to the Bell Laboratories in 1956, the laboratory work waned. I am not an experimentalist. Another colleague, Theodore M. Alfred, and I continued a comparative study of the operation of management development programs in a number of large companies. The subjects were a group of former Sloan Fellows, but our studies ranged widely within their companies as we sought to learn more about the way in which theories and practices within different organizations influence the making of managers.

These studies are not yet complete, but this book has grown out of them and is to a large extent the fruit of Mr. Sloan's questions and the opportunity to pursue them afforded by the Alfred P. Sloan Foundation.

It seems clear to me that the making of managers, in so far as they are made, is only to a rather small degree the result of management's formal efforts in management development. It is to a much greater degree the result of management's conception of the nature of its task and of all the policies and practices which are constructed to implement this conception. The way a business is managed determines to a very large extent what people are perceived to have "potential" and how they develop. We go off on the wrong track when we seek to study management development in terms of the formal machinery of programs carrying this label.

Without in the least minimizing the importance of the work that has been done to improve the selection of people with managerial potential, I have come to the conviction that some of our most important problems lie elsewhere. Even if we possessed methods enabling us to do a perfect job of selecting young men with the capacity to become top executives, the practical gain for industry would be negligible under today's conditions. The reason is that we have not learned enough about the utilization of talent, about the creation of an organizational climate conducive to human growth. The blunt fact is that we are a long way from realizing the potential represented by the human resources we now recruit into industry. We have much to accomplish with respect to utilization before further improvements in selection will become important.

This volume is an attempt to substantiate the thesis that the human side of enterprise is "all of a piece"—that the theoretical assumptions management holds about controlling its human re-sources determine the whole character of the enterprise. They de-termine also the quality of its successive generations of manage-ment.

Of course the process is circular, and herein lies the possibility and the hope of future progress. The key question for top manage-ment is: "What are your assumptions (implicit as well as explicit) about the most effective way to manage people?" From the answer to this question flow the answers to the questions Mr. Sloan raised in our discussion about the making of managers, as well as answers to many other questions which perplex and confound management as it seeks to achieve more successfully the economic objectives of enterprise. It will be clear to the reader that I believe many of our present assumptions about the most effective way to manage people are far from adequate.

It is completely impossible for me to acknowledge individually the help I have received in evolving the ideas presented here. Many professional colleagues, past and present, and many close friends in management have encouraged, criticized, and inspired me for twenty years. I cannot hold them responsible for what is in this volume, but they taught me most of what I now believe I know about management, about social science, and about the relevance of the latter to the former.

I have tried to protect the anonymity of the companies from which illustrative materials have been drawn. May I, however, acknowledge with deep gratitude the time given to Mr. Alfred and me by some thirty former Sloan Fellows and more than a hundred managers in their companies to answer our questions, the frankness with which they were answered, and the interest these men took in our studies.

To Patricia Macpherson, my secretary, I owe much. Were it not for her cheerful patience with innumerable rewritings and editings, this book would never have been completed.

Finally, to the Alfred P. Sloan Foundation, and to Mr. Sloan personally, my sincere thanks, not only for the funds which made this book possible but for the freedom to pursue my not always intelligible interests where they led.

Douglas McGregor

CONTENTS

Preface . . . .   **v**

Part One. The Theoretical Assumptions of Management . .   **1**

   1. Management and Scientific Knowledge . . .   **3**
   2. Methods of Influence and Control **15**
   3. Theory X: The Traditional View of Direction and
      Control **33**
   4. Theory Y: The Integration of Individual and Organi-
      zational Goals **45**

Part Two. Theory Y in Practice **59**

   5. Management by Integration and Self-control . .   **61**
   6. A Critique of Performance Appraisal **77**
   7. Administering Salaries and Promotions **90**
   8. The Scanlon Plan **110**
   9. Participation in Perspective **124**
  10. The Managerial Climate **132**
  11. Staff-Line Relationships **145**
  12. Improving Staff-Line Collaboration . . .   **157**

X   CONTENTS

Part Three. The Development of Managerial Talent . . . 177

   13. An Analysis of Leadership 179
   14. Management Development Programs 190
   15. Acquiring Managerial Skills in the Classroom . . 207
   16. The Managerial Team 227

Conclusion 244

PART ONE: THE THEORETICAL ASSUMPTIONS OF MANAGEMENT

1

Management and Scientific Knowledge

Every professional is concerned with the use of knowledge in the achievement of objectives: the engineer as he designs equipment, the medical practitioner as he diagnoses and prescribes for the ills of his patients, the lawyer or the architect as he serves his clients. The professional draws upon the knowledge of science and of his colleagues, and upon knowledge gained through personal experience. The degree to which he relies upon the first two of these rather than the third is one of the ways in which the professional may be distinguished from the layman.

It is beginning to be possible for the industrial manager to be a professional in this respect. He can draw upon a reasonable and growing body of knowledge in the social sciences as an aid to achieving his managerial objectives. He need not rely exclusively on personal experience and observation.

Progress in any profession is associated with the ability to predict and control, and this is true also of industrial management. One of the major tasks of management is to organize human effort in the service of the economic objectives of the enterprise.

Every managerial decision has behavioral consequences. Successful management depends—not alone, but significantly—upon the ability to predict and control human behavior.

Our ability along these lines today is spotty. It is remarkably good in some respects. Consider such everyday acts as making an appointment, signing a purchase agreement, placing a long-distance call, asking a subordinate to prepare a report, making a hotel reservation, mailing a letter. In literally thousands of ways we predict with a high degree of accuracy what others will do, and we control their behavior in the sense that our actions lead to the desired consequences.

At the same time, it is true that other attempts at prediction and control are quite inadequate. Many of the important social problems of our time reflect this inadequacy: juvenile delinquency, crime, the high traffic fatality rate, management-labor conflict, the cold war.

The results so far achieved in the management of business and industry reflect considerable ability to predict and control human behavior. The fact that a company is economically successful means, among other things, that management has been able to attract people into the organization and to organize and direct their efforts toward the production and sale of goods or services at a profit. Nevertheless, few managers are satisfied with their ability to predict and control the behavior of the members of their organizations. The interest expressed in new developments in this field is an indication of management's recognition of the opportunity for improvement. The frequent success of the outright charlatan in peddling managerial patent medicines also reflects the consciousness of inadequacy. Many managers would agree that the effectiveness of their organizations would be at least doubled if they could discover how to tap the unrealized potential present in their human resources.

I share with some of my colleagues the conviction that the social sciences could contribute more effectively than they have to managerial progress with respect to the human side of enterprise. There are, of course, many reasons why improvement has been slow. Some have to do with the social sciences themselves: they are still in their adolescence in comparison with the physical sciences; their findings are piecemeal and scattered; they lack precision; many critical issues are still in controversy. These are relative matters, however. One need only contrast the situation today with that thirty years ago to recognize that much has been accomplished. The social sciences are a rich resource today for management even though they have not reached full maturity.

I am not particularly impressed with arguments that social scientists do not publish their findings in language intelligible to the layman. Neither do physicists! Also, while it is lamentable that some social scientists jump incautiously from relatively precarious theory to practical applications, and others refuse to concern themselves at all with applications, there is nothing unique about social science in these respects. Today most managers are forced to rely on "middlemen" in the form of social scientist consultants or staff, or on literature intermediate between scientific journals and the Sunday supplements to interpret theory and research or to help them judge the scientific adequacy of claims or proposals. The time is not far off when the competent manager—like any other professional practitioner—will find it a necessity to be well enough versed in the scientific disciplines relevant to this work to be able to read the literature and judge the adequacy of scientific findings and claims.

This is not to say that we social scientists can ignore our responsibilities. It is to say that the position of the manager vis-à-vis the social sciences will one day be no different than that of the engineer vis-à-vis the physical sciences or the doctor vis-à-vis chemistry or biology. The professional need not be a scientist, but he must be sophisticated enough to make competent use of scientific knowledge,

Every Managerial Act Rests on Theory

There are some other reasons why management has been relatively slow to utilize social science knowledge. Two of these are especially important. The first is that every manager quite naturally considers himself his own social scientist. His personal experience with people from childhood on has been so rich that he feels little real need to turn elsewhere for knowledge of human behavior. The social scientist's knowledge often appears to him to be theoretical and unrelated to the realities with which he must deal, whereas his own experience-based knowledge is practical and useful.

This frequent, invidious comparison of the practical and the theoretical with respect to the management of human resources has been a severe handicap to progress in this field. It has led to premature and misguided attempts to translate scientific findings into action; it has permitted the quack and the charlatan to peddle worthless gimmicks and programs.

Every managerial act rests on assumptions, generalizations, and hypotheses—that is to say, on theory. Our assumptions are frequently implicit, sometimes quite unconscious, often conflicting; nevertheless, they determine our predictions that if we do *a*, *b* will occur. Theory and practice are inseparable.

Next time you attend a management staff meeting at which a policy problem is under discussion or some action is being considered, try a variant on the pastime of doodling. Jot down the assumptions (beliefs, opinions, convictions, generalizations) about human behavior made during the discussion by the participants. Some of these will be explicitly stated ("A manager must himself be technically competent in a given field in order to manage professionals within it."). Most will be implicit, but fairly easily inferred ("We should require the office force to punch time clocks as they do in the factory."). It will not make too much difference whether the problem under discussion is a human problem, a financial or a technical one. Tune your ear to listen for assumptions about human behavior, whether they relate to an individual, a particular group, or people in general. The length and variety of your list will surprise you.

It is possible to have more or less adequate theoretical assumptions; it is not possible to reach a managerial decision or take a managerial action uninfluenced by assumptions, whether adequate or not. The insistence on being practical really means, "Let's accept *my* theoretical assumptions without argument or test." The common practice of proceeding without explicit examination of theoretical assumptions leads, at times, to remarkable inconsistencies in managerial behavior.

A manager, for example, states that he delegates to his subordinates. When asked, he expresses assumptions such as, "People need to learn to take responsibility," or, "Those closer to the situation can make the best decisions." However, he has arranged to obtain a constant flow of detailed information about the behavior of his subordinates, and he uses this information to police their behavior and to "second-guess" their decisions. He says, "I am held responsible, so I need to know what is going on." He sees no inconsistency in his behavior, nor does he recognize some other assumptions which are implicit: "People can't be trusted," or, "They can't really make as good decisions as I can."

With one hand, and in accord with certain assumptions, he delegates; with the other, and in line with other assumptions, he takes actions which have the effect of nullifying his delegation. Not only does he fail to recognize the inconsistencies involved, but if faced with them he is likely to deny them.

Another common way of denying the importance of theory to managerial behavior is to insist that management is an art. This also precludes critical examination of the theoretical assumptions underlying managerial actions by placing reliance on intuitions and feelings, which are by definition not subject to question. The issue is not whether management is a science. It is not. Its purposes are different. Science is concerned with the advancement of knowledge; management, like any profession, is concerned with the achievement of practical objectives. The issue is whether management can utilize scientific knowledge in the achievement of those objectives. To insist that management is an art is frequently no more than a denial of the relevance of systematic, tested knowledge to practice. So long as the manager fails to question the validity of his personal assumptions, he is unlikely to avail himself of what is available in science. And much is there. The knowledge in the social sciences is not sparse, but frequently it contradicts personal experience and threatens some cherished illusions. The easy way out is rejection, since one can always find imperfections and inadequacies in scientific knowledge.

Control Is Selective Adaptation

An equally important reason for management's failure to make effective use of current social science knowledge has to do with a misconception concerning the nature of control in the field of human behavior. In engineering, control consists in adjustment to natural law. It does not mean making nature do our bidding. We do not, for example, dig channels in the expectation that water will flow uphill; we do not use kerosene to put out a fire. In designing an internal combustion engine we recognize and adjust to the fact that gases expand when heated; we do not attempt to make them behave otherwise. With respect to physical phenomena, control involves the selection of means which are *appropriate* to the nature of the phenomena with which we are concerned.

In the human field the situation is the same, but we often dig channels to make water flow uphill. Many of our attempts to control behavior, far from representing selective adaptations, are in direct violation of human nature. They consist in trying to make people behave as we wish without concern for natural law. Yet we can no more expect to achieve desired results through inappropriate action in this field than in engineering.

Individual incentive plans provide a good example of an attempt to control behavior which fails to take sufficient account of "natural law"—in this case, human behavior in the industrial setting.

The practical logic of incentives is that people want money, and that they will work harder to get more of it. In accord with this logic, we measure jobs, establish standards for "a fair day's work," and determine a scale of incentive pay which provides a bonus for productivity above the standard.

Incentive plans do not, however, take account of several other well-demonstrated characteristics of behavior in the organizational setting: (1) that most people also want the approval of their fellow workers and that, if necessary, they will forego increased pay to obtain this approval; (2) that no managerial assurances can persuade workers that incentive rates will remain inviolate regardless of how much they produce; (3) that the ingenuity of the average worker is sufficient to outwit *any* system of controls devised by management.

A "good" individual incentive plan may bring about a moderate increase in productivity (perhaps 15 per cent), but it also may bring a considerable variety of protective behaviors—deliberate restriction of output, hidden jigs and fixtures, hidden production, fudged records, grievances over rates and standards, etc. In addition, it generally creates attitudes which are the opposite of those desired—antagonism toward those who administer the plan, cynicism with respect to management's integrity and fairness, indifference to the importance of collaboration with other parts of the organization (except for collusive efforts to *defeat* the incentive system).

All of these results are costly, and so are the managerial countermeasures which must be established to combat them (staff effort, elaborate control procedures, closer supervision, concessions with respect to rates, down-time provisions, setup arrangements, etc.). If the *total* costs of administering the incentive program—both direct and indirect—were calculated, it would often turn out that they add up to more than the total gains from increased productivity. Certainly the typical incentive plan is of limited effectiveness as a method of control if the purpose is to motivate human beings to direct their efforts toward organizational objectives.

Another fallacy is often revealed in managerial attempts to control human behavior. When we fail to achieve the results we desire, we tend to seek the cause everywhere but where it usually lies: in our choice of inappropriate methods of control. The engineer does not blame water for flowing downhill rather than up, nor gases for expanding rather than contracting when heated. However, when people respond to managerial decisions in undesired ways, the normal response is to blame them. It is *their* stupidity, or *their* uncooperativeness, or *their* laziness which is seized on as the explanation of what happened, not management's failure to select appropriate means for control.

The director of operations research in a large company is concerned because fewer than half of the solutions to operating problems developed by his research team have been adopted by the line organization. He is currently trying to persuade higher management to issue orders to the line regarding the implementation of certain of his findings. "If they can't recognize what's good for the organization, they will have to be told what to do," is his conclusion. Not only is his assumption of the line's stupidity incorrect, but so also is his further assumption that commands from higher management will solve the problem. Yet, for him, the whole problem is "out there." It does not occur to him to question his own methods of control.

Effective prediction and control are as central to the task of management as they are to the task of engineering or of medicine. If we would improve our ability to organize and direct human effort toward economic ends, we must not only recognize that this is so, we must also recognize and correct some common fallacies with respect to these matters.

Human behavior is predictable, but, as in physical science, accurate prediction hinges on the correctness of underlying theoretical assumptions. There is, in fact, no prediction without theory; all managerial decisions and actions rest on assumptions about behavior. If we adopt the posture of the ostrich with respect to our assumptions under the mistaken idea that we are thus "being practical," or that "management is an art," our progress with respect to the human side of enterprise will indeed be slow. Only as we examine and test our theoretical assumptions can we hope to make them more adequate, to remove inconsistencies, and thus to improve our ability to predict.

We can improve our ability to control only if we recognize that control consists in selective adaptation to human nature rather than in attempting to make human nature conform to our wishes. If our attempts to control are unsuccessful, the cause generally lies in our choice of inappropriate means. We will be unlikely to improve our managerial competence by blaming people for failing to behave according to our predictions.

Control and Professional Ethics

Discussions of the idea of controlling human behavior raise justifiable apprehensions about possible manipulation and exploitation. These concerns are not new, but they will be intensified as the manager becomes more professional in his use of social science knowledge to achieve the objectives of the economic enterprise. We must pause, therefore, to consider another characteristic of the professional: his conscious concern with ethical values.

Scientific knowledge is indifferent with respect to its uses. In this sense (and only in this sense) science is independent of values. Scientific knowledge can be used for good or evil purposes; it can be used to help mankind or to destroy him, as we have seen so dramatically in recent times with respect to certain applications of nuclear physics. It is obvious, therefore, that the more professional the manager becomes in his use of scientific knowledge, the more professional he must become in his sensitivity to ethical values. He must be concerned both with broad social values and with those involved in his attempts to control the members of his own organization.

Management's freedom to manage has been progressively curtailed in our society during the past century. Legislation with respect to child labor, the employment of women, workmen's compensation, collective bargaining, and many other matters reflects society's concern with the ethics of management. One approach to these problems is to see all restrictions on management as unreasonable and to fight blindly against them. This was fairly typical of industrial management a generation or two ago. The other approach is to become more sensitive to human values and to exert self-control through a positive, conscious, ethical code. It is this latter approach which characterizes the concept of the "social responsibility" of management about which we hear so much today.

Even though some managers are increasingly aware of these problems and are making sincere attempts to keep their behavior in line with high ethical principles, we have a way to go before the ethics of management are comparable to those, for example, of medicine. There are many instances in which essentially unethical practices are either ignored or defended with rationalizations.

It is usual today for big corporations to encourage, and sometimes to require, their executives to have annual physical examinations. Not many years ago it was common practice to make the data from these examinations available to top management to use in making decisions affecting the individual's career. Today, most large companies have a firm policy that these personal data about the individual are shared by the doctor only with the patient himself. It is up to the individual executive whether he will make this information known to his superiors. Most managements today are scrupulous in observing this policy.

Contrast this practice with that used in psychological testing and in the clinical diagnosis of the personalities of executives for purposes of placement. The reference here is not to initial selection but to administrative practices affecting the career of the individual after he has become an accepted member of the organization.

The data obtained from such tests and clinical interviews are private information which the individual gives about himself unwittingly. He has, in effect, no choice, since he does not know what significance will be placed upon his responses by the test or the interviewer. To use such data for administrative purposes seems quite clearly to be as much an invasion of individual rights as to use medical data in this way. Yet, many companies have opposite policies with respect to these two kinds of information.

It is natural to expect management to be committed to the economic objectives of the industrial organization. However, the history of social legislation has indicated that society will grant management freedom in its pursuit of these objectives only to the extent that human values are preserved and protected. Professions like medicine, education, and law in general maintain high ethical standards with respect to the influences they exert on human beings. In directing the human resources of the industrial organization, management is in a similar position. Here, as elsewhere in our society, the price of freedom is responsibility.

REFERENCES

Drucker, Peter F., "Thinking Ahead: The Potentials of Management Science," *Harvard Business Review,* vol. 37, no. 1 (January–February), 1959.

Gouldner, Alvin W., "Theoretical Requirements of the Applied Social Sciences," *American Sociological Review,* vol. 22, 1957, pp. 91–102.

Selekman, Benjamin M., "Sin Bravely: The Danger of Perfectionism," *Harvard Business Review,* vol. 37, no. 1 (January–February), 1959.

Wilensky, Harold L., "Human Relations in the Workplace: An Appraisal of Some Recent Research," *Research in Industrial Human Relations.* New York: Harper & Brothers, 1957, pp. 25–50.

2

Methods of Influence and Control

Formal theories of organization have been taught in management courses for many years, and there is an extensive literature on the subject. The textbook principles of organization—hierarchical structure, authority, unity of command, task specialization, division of staff and line, span of control, equality of responsibility and authority, etc.—comprise a logically persuasive set of assumptions which have had a profound influence upon managerial behavior over several generations. Despite the fact that they rest primarily on armchair speculation rather than on empirical research, the literature gives the impression that these classical principles are beyond challenge. (The manual for a supervisory training program in one large company suggests that the instructor point out by analogy and example that the principles of organization are "like the laws of physics.")

Formal textbook principles have blended into personal assumptions in many ways. In some instances the formal theory has been consistent with these assumptions; sometimes there have been sharp inconsistencies. Since it is rare for deep-rooted emotional

15

convictions to be abandoned in favor of conflicting academic theory, at least in the field of the social sciences, some managers simply reject the formal principles (and the "long-haired" professors who propound them) and retain their own assumptions. In other instances there are varying degrees of accommodation between academic theory and personal conviction. Out of this process of rejection and accommodation have come many innovations, some of which have been successful. It is not difficult, in fact, to find examples which contradict almost every one of the textbook principles of organization. The arguments with respect to these exceptions are naturally vehement, but regardless of their merit, it is becoming clear that the traditional principles fall considerably short of being like the laws of physics. Among many reasons, three are especially significant:

1. The conventional principles were derived primarily from the study of models (the military and the Catholic Church) which differ in important respects from modern industrial organizations. It is a plausible idea that there should be universal principles of organization, and that they could be derived from the study of such old and successful institutions. However, if there are universal principles common to all forms of organization, it is now apparent that they are not the ones derived by classical theorists from the Church and the military. As an example, unity of command (the principle that each member of an organization must only have one boss) may be essential on the battlefield, but it is not a universal principle. Whatever the organization chart may show, the typical middle-level manager in the modern industrial organization finds that his behavior is controlled not by one but by several "superiors." In some companies, project groups are formed to carry out complex tasks, and the members of these groups report both to the project supervisor and

to their functional superiors. Moreover, there is one organization where subordinates always have had two bosses: the family!

2. Classical organization theory suffers from "ethnocentrism": It ignores the significance of the political, social, and economic milieu in shaping organizations and influencing managerial practice. We live today in a world which only faintly resembles that of a half century ago. The standard of living, the level of education, and the political complexion of the United States today profoundly affect both the possibilities and limitations of organizational behavior. In addition, technological changes are bringing about changes in all types of organization. In the military, for example, it is becoming increasingly difficult to manage a weapons team in the field as a typical infantry unit was managed a couple of decades ago. Such a team requires a high degree of autonomy. Instead of following explicit orders from superiors, it must be able to adjust its behavior to fit local circumstances within the context of relatively broad objectives. (It is interesting to note the attempts that are made—by "programming" for example—to retain central control over the operations of such units. Established theories of control are not abandoned easily, even in the face of clear evidence of their inappropriateness.)

3. Underlying the principles of classical organization theory are a number of assumptions about human behavior which are at best only partially true. In this respect organizational theory is in much the same state today as was economic theory at the turn of the century. Knowledge accumulated during recent decades challenges and contradicts assumptions which are still axiomatic in conventional organization theory. It will be necessary to examine some of these assumptions in detail.

Unfortunately, those classical principles of organization—derived from inappropriate models, unrelated to the political, social, economic, and technological milieu, and based on erroneous assumptions about behavior—continue to influence our thinking about the management of the human resources of industry. Management's attempts to solve the problems arising from the inadequacy of these assumptions have often involved the search for new formulas, new techniques, new procedures. These generally yield disappointing results because they are adjustments to symptoms rather than causes. The real need is for new theory, changed assumptions, more understanding of the nature of human behavior in organizational settings.

Methods of Influence

If there is a single assumption which pervades conventional organizational theory it is that authority is the central, indispensable means of managerial control. This is the basic principle of organization in the textbook theory of management. The very structure of the organization is a hierarchy of authoritative relationships. The terms *up* and *down* within the structure refer to a scale of authority. Most of the other principles of organization, such as unity of command, staff and line, span of control, are directly derived from this one.

The first thing to be noted about authority is that it is but one of several forms of social influence or control. Direct physical coercion is the most powerful and the most primitive of these. It was almost universal a few centuries ago, and we still resort to it sometimes, although its use is limited by social prohibitions in our culture today. Physical coercion is a legitimate means of social control over certain forms of criminal behavior; it occurs occasionally in severe labor disputes; and it is common in parental control of small children. We are devoting a substantial portion of our national budget today to prevent its most frightening use: in war.

Persuasion, in its many forms, represents another means of social control. In the sales field, where authority and physical coercion are clearly inappropriate, we place major reliance on this type of influence. Within management, consultation and discussion provide at least a partial substitution of persuasion for authority. In certain kinds of relationships, but not in others, there is the expectation that authority or even physical coercion will be resorted to if persuasion is ineffective. This situation is common in labor relations and in the international field. Within industrial organizations, managers frequently speak euphemistically of "selling" an idea or a course of action to someone when both parties are fully aware that if persuasion is not successful resort will be had to authority as the means of control. In a genuine sales relationship one cannot fall back on authority if persuasion fails. This makes quite a difference!

Finally, there is the form of influence involved in professional "help." While the nature of this influence is relatively poorly understood, it is different from ordinary methods of persuasion. Most professionals—lawyers, doctors, architects, engineers—simply rely on "the authority of knowledge." Their relationships with clients represent an extreme form of authoritarianism in which "help" is conceived in completely unilateral terms. They are often indifferent to the fact that the client can ignore their advice, or even terminate the relationship, at will.

True professional help, as typified by the exceptionally sophisticated and sensitive individual in any professional field, does not consist in playing God with the client, but in placing the professional's knowledge and skill at the client's disposal. It is a particularly important form of social influence which is not at all well understood. We will have occasion to examine its nature in some detail in Chapters 5 and 12.

All these methods of social control are relative; none is absolute. The appropriateness of a given form of control is a function of several other variables. Effective control consists in "selective adaptations" to these variables. The engineer does not dig channels to make water flow uphill; the salesman does not give commands to a customer; the superintendent does not give orders to the president; a nation at war does not offer professional help to the enemy; the parent does not give advice to his year-old child.

The success of any form of social influence or control depends ultimately upon altering the ability of others to achieve their goals or satisfy their needs. The modification may be an enhancement of this ability (for example, through the offer of a product, the provision of professional advice, or the promise of a reward) or a curtailment of it (for example, through a disciplinary action, a jail sentence, the termination of employment, or the threat of a punishment). Such modifications in the ability of the individual to achieve goals or satisfy needs may be relatively minor (as is the case with product advertising in mass media) or major (as is the case with the superior in an organizational relationship who may affect the long-term career expectations of his subordinates in important ways). However, in either case, the influence can occur only when there is some degree of dependence of the one party on the other. The dependence may be quite small or very great, it may be unilateral or mutual, but if there is no dependence there is no opportunity to control. Unless I perceive that you can somehow affect my ability to satisfy my needs, you cannot influence my behavior.

Thus the nature and degree of dependence is a critical factor in determining what methods of control will be effective. Selective adaptation to these aspects of organizational relationships is a matter of great importance. Let us consider in a little more detail what this means.

The Limitations of Authority

In general, both the literature on organization and management practice accept authority as an absolute rather than a relative concept. Little recognition is given to control as a process of selective adaptation to such varying conditions as the nature and degree of dependence in organizational relationships. The consequences are of considerable significance. Some of our most troublesome problems in managing the human resources of industry in the United States today are directly traceable to the assumption that authority is an absolute and to inappropriate attempts to control behavior which flow from this assumption.

The effectiveness of authority as a means of control depends first of all upon the ability to enforce it through the use of punishment. In the two organizations which have been the models for classical organization theory, the situation with respect to enforcement is clear. In the military, authority is enforceable through the court-martial, with the death penalty as the extreme form of punishment. In the Church, excommunication represents the psychological equivalent of the death penalty.

A half century or more ago, industrial management had, in the threat of unemployment, a form of punishment which made the use of authority relatively effective. Discharge as the ultimate punishment was even further reinforced by yellow-dog contracts and employer blacklists. The situation today is vastly different. The social legislation of the 1930s, unemployment compensation, the limitations on arbitrary discharge brought about by a generation of widespread collective bargaining, and the far greater mobility of our citizens all serve to make discharge a considerably less severe form of punishment than it once was. As a means of enforcing authority it is certainly not comparable to excommunication from the Church or to the military court-martial.

What this indicates is that the employment relationship involves substantially less dependence than it did a half century ago. Alternative relationships, alternative ways of satisfying needs and achieving goals are sufficiently available that a particular employment relationship can be terminated with a relatively smaller loss. Moreover, the dependence is further reduced by the various negotiated limitations on management's freedom to exercise the authority to discharge.

This phenomenon of decreased dependence in social relationships is not confined entirely to industry. Consider, for example, what has happened in the last fifty years in the United States to the position of the wife in the marital relationship, or of the older adolescent child in the family. We have tended to recognize more readily in these relationships the effect of lessened dependence upon the appropriateness of authority as a means of social control. The significance of the parallel change in the employment relationship—within management or between the worker and management—has been less well understood.

The second limitation upon the effectiveness of authority as a means of control is the availability of countermeasures. These can range, depending upon conditions, from a minimal but relatively ineffective compliance to open rebellion. The elaborate legalism of certain collective bargaining relationships provides one illustration of the use of countermeasures to render authority less effective. Likewise, restriction of output, featherbedding, and other more subtle forms of sabotage of organizational objectives are symptoms which suggest that management leans on a weak crutch if it relies too much on authority today. Moreover, these countermeasures are not limited to workers or to unionized plants. Although given different labels, restriction of output and featherbedding can often be observed within management! They are not unknown even at the vice-presidential level.

Less obvious, but equally effective in defeating managerial purposes, are such things as indifference to organizational objectives, low standards of performance, ingenious forms of protective behavior, and refusal to accept responsibility. The fact is that these phenomena are so familiar that most managers tend in daily practice to rely less and less on the exercise of personal authority except in the crisis situation when other methods fail. This becomes more evident the higher one goes in the organization. The use of commands and orders within the higher levels of management is relatively rare. This was not true fifty or even twenty-five years ago.

The outstanding fact about relationships in the modern industrial organization is that they involve a high degree of *interde*pendence. Not only are subordinates dependent upon those above them in the organization for satisfying their needs and achieving their goals, but managers at every level are dependent upon all those below them for achieving both their own and organizational goals.

An agent of the Textile Workers Union of America likes to tell the story of the occasion when a new manager appeared in the mill where he was working. The manager came into the weave room the day he arrived. He walked directly over to the agent and said, "Are you Belloc?" The agent acknowledged that he was. The manager said, "I am the new manager here. When I manage a mill, I run it. Do you understand?" The agent nodded, and then waved his hand. The workers, intently watching this encounter, shut down every loom in the room immediately. The agent turned to the manager and said, "All right, go ahead and run it."

This is a dramatic illustration of the fact that every manager at every level is dependent upon those below him in the organization. The dependence may be more pronounced—it is certainly more explicit—when those below are organized in a militant union. It is nevertheless a fact whether or not workers are formally organized, and within the management framework as well. The trouble with focusing explicitly on the concept of authority is that it blinds us to this dependence downwards. Some people are strongly motivated toward the managerial role because they perceive it as an escape from dependence. Their reliance on authority, their attempted escape, tends in fact to be self-defeating.

Interdependence in organizations involves more than dependence upward and downward; it also involves lateral dependence. Interdependence is characteristic of staff-line relationships. It is equally characteristic of relationships between many line departments (particularly where the output of one department is the input of another), and it is characteristic of the relationship among any group of subordinates who report to a common boss. The competition which is so common within such a group for power and position and recognition is a reflection of the interdependence inherent in the situation.

Conventional organization theory gives full recognition to dependence upward, but it fails to recognize the significance of interdependence. This is a result again of the theorist's choice of models. The Church as an organization rests on dependence which is essentially one-way. The ultimate source of all authority and all power is God, and all members of the organization are, therefore, dependent upward. In the military—under the conditions of war which are the conditions for which the military organization is built—individuals are required to sacrifice their personal goals and needs to the necessities of the national crisis, and to accept dependence upward. As we have noted above, both these organizations have a means of reinforcing this dependence.

Industry, on the other hand, is the economic organ of society, of all of us. Its ultimate purpose is to serve the common good. There is no superhuman source of authority; there is no sound basis for expecting the individual to sacrifice his personal goals or needs for the organization (except possibly under crisis conditions), and there is no successful way to enforce this expectation if it does exist. In a free enterprise society such as ours there is no final sanction that can be applied to enforce managerial authority. In fact, because the dependence is mutual, sanctions can be applied in both directions. Management can attempt to enforce its authority through disciplinary action, but the individual can re-sign; he can join a powerful union; he can resort to a variety of tactics which influence the ability of those above him to satisfy *their* needs and to fulfill their responsibilities to the organization. They are dependent upon him, just as he is dependent upon them.

It is fundamental, therefore, to any theory of organization that the nature of the dependency relationships be understood and al-lowed for. In the social, economic, and political milieu of the United States today the management of industry is becoming un-able to rely on authority as the sole, or even the primary, method of accomplishing organizational objectives through people. Its de-pendence downward is too great to permit this unilateral means of control.

The curve in Figure 1 is a rough schematic representation of the way in which the appropriateness of authority probably varies as a function of dependence. When the dependence in the relation-ship is relatively complete (as in a slave economy or between a parent and a small child), authority can be used almost exclusively

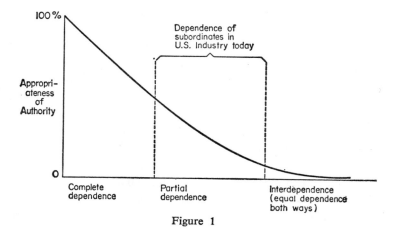

Figure 1

without fear of negative consequences. At the other extreme, when dependence is approximately equal, authority is useless as a means of control (consider the relationship between friends, for example).

In United States industry today, employees are in a relationship of partial dependence. Authority, as a means of influence, is certainly not useless, but for many purposes it is less appropriate than persuasion or professional help. Exclusive reliance upon authority encourages countermeasures, minimal performance, even open rebellion. The dependence—as in the case of the adolescent in the family—is simply not great enough to guarantee compliance.

The Psychology of Dependence

One of the reasons why these limitations on the effectiveness of authority are not so well recognized as one would expect is that dependence involves deep-seated emotional reactions. To be dependent is in some ways satisfying. It is nice to be taken care of, to be secure. In other ways it is frustrating. To be dependent is to be limited in freedom, to be subject to influences which are frequently perceived as arbitrary and unjust.

Likewise, independence is satisfying. It is nice to be able to stand on one's own feet, make one's own decisions, lead one's own life. On the other hand, independence can be threatening. One can be too far out on a limb; the risks can be frightening.

These emotional concomitants of dependence and independence stem from a series of universal human experiences. Each of us is born into a relationship of relatively complete dependence. As infants and small children we would not survive unless we were taken care of completely. The process of growing up involves a gradual shift out of this state of dependence as we become able to take more and more responsibility for ourselves.

The end product, however, is not independence. No individual in society is completely independent. *Inter*dependence is a central characteristic of the modern, complex society. In every aspect of life we depend upon each other in achieving our goals. We do not grow our own food, make our own clothes, provide our own transportation or shelter, educate ourselves. We have learned that as a society we can have more of everything we want by specializing individually. However, the price of specialization is dependence on others.

Growing up and learning to live in this complex of interdependent relationships is not without its emotional conflicts. Our contrary emotional needs and anxieties are profoundly influential. No matter how we resolve them as we grow up, we remain sensitive when we are placed in a situation which resembles, even remotely, the dependence of infancy. To be a subordinate in an organization is to be placed in a dependent relationship which has enough of the elements of the earlier one to be sensitive and, under certain conditions, explosive.

The desirable end of the growth process is an ability to strike a balance—to tolerate certain forms of dependence without being unduly frustrated, and at the same time to stand alone in some respects without undue anxiety. Some of us never learn to tolerate even a moderate amount of dependence with comfort. We remain rebellious; any hint of the exercise of personal authority over us is threatening. Others of us tend to be unhappy if we are too much on our own. We like to lean on those above and to be sure of some degree of protection and security. The variations in these patterns are, of course, infinite. Whatever they are, few of us achieve that degree of emotional maturity which makes us able to accept dependence with complete objectivity. Dependent relationships are sensitive ones.

Role Relationships

The common-sense assumption is that the managerial relationship is essentially a single, uniform one. We tend to think that the boss is a boss is a boss is a boss. This is not the case at all. The circumstances change from hour to hour and from day to day as the manager undertakes different activities, and the methods of influence which are appropriate shift accordingly.

In describing all forms of social relationships, we tend to attach labels which define their more obvious characteristics and which assign to the parties single and unchanging roles. Thus we speak of the parent, the husband, the friend, the manager. In each of these, however, the individual occupies a variety of different roles over time. The parent, for example, may at times be a playmate, at other times a teacher, at other times an arbitrator, at other times a protector. The parent's behavior and the forms of influence he utilizes shift appreciably as the conditions demand different roles.

The same thing is true of the manager. At times he may be in the role of the leader of a group of subordinates; at other times he may be a member of a group of his peers. Sometimes he is in the role of teacher; at other times he may be a decision maker, a disciplinarian, a helper, a consultant, or simply an observer. When he is helping a subordinate to analyze a problem and decide how to deal with it, the methods he uses to influence the subordinate will be quite different than when he is dealing with a disciplinary problem. The very nature of the relation shifts as the circumstances change. Moreover, the manager adopts different roles as he deals with the manager of another department, or with his immediate superior, or with a superior several levels higher in the organization.

The managerial role is not a single, invariant one, but a complex of different roles. Ordinarily we adjust to the changing circumstances without conscious thought, but an observer will detect major changes in behavior and attitude, and in the resulting behavior of the other party to the relationship. Conventional theories of organization do not recognize the significance of role flexibility in the managerial relationship.

The degree of flexibility in managerial roles which would be most appropriate in influencing behavior is limited not only by the manager's own theoretical assumptions and attitudes but by the expectations of his subordinates. They, too, tend to make the common-sense assumption that a boss is a boss is a boss. The formal position which the superior occupies in the organizational hierarchy and the emphasis upon authority as *the* managerial method of influence make it difficult for subordinates to perceive and respond to a boss as a colleague or as a consultant. Only if the manager is genuinely sensitive to the differing role requirements, and is in addition explicit about the role he is adopting, can subordinates learn to respond appropriately. The latter are sometimes considerably confused when a boss who has consistently occupied a single authoritarian role in all his dealings with them suddenly becomes "participative" without making explicit his own conscious attempt to shift his role.

Despite these difficulties, it is clear that the circumstances of the superior-subordinate relationship do shift in ways which demand considerable role flexibility. If we accept the theoretical hypothesis that appropriate control is a function of the conditions, we cannot ignore its implications.

Of course, there are times when the role of boss is the only appropriate one. It is sometimes necessary to issue a direct order, to take a formal disciplinary action, to terminate a subordinate's employment. There are other instances, however, where we tend unnecessarily to think of the boss role as inevitable. A superior acting explicitly as an "arbitrator" in resolving an issue between subordinates, or in deciding upon one course of action among several proposed alternatives is in a role which can carry quite different overtones for subordinates than if the superior is inflexible in his role of boss.

The necessity for role flexibility sometimes places the manager in an impossible situation. This happens when he is forced to occupy incompatible roles in a relationship with another individual or a group. Performance appraisal programs, for example, often require the superior to occupy simultaneously the role of judge and the role of counselor to a subordinate. Members of staff departments are frequently required to be specialists offering professional service and advice, and *in addition,* policemen administering managerial controls.

Obviously, circumstances which force incompatible roles on the individual create tension and confusion in the relationship. The consequent costs for the organization may be substantial. We will have occasion to examine these problems of role incompatibility further in Chapter 6, and again in Chapter 12 when we consider staff-line relationships.

From Physical Coercion to Selective Adaptation

For all of these reasons, it would appear that authority is an inappropriate method of control on which to place exclusive reliance in United States industry today if management's purpose is to influence behavior toward the achievement of organizational objectives. It is obvious that it cannot be dispensed with altogether. Under certain circumstances it may be essential, but for promoting collaboration it is at best a weak crutch.

Over the long sweep of history there have been two major transitions with respect to the central means of controlling human behavior in organizational settings. The first was the transition from sheer physical force to reliance on formal authority. It took centuries. Even today we tend to slip back into reliance on force when other attempts to influence fail. The transition is clearly further along in the United States and Western Europe than it is in some parts of the world. At the level of international relations, it is evident that we have only a precarious foothold on the transitional ladder from primitive force to "higher" forms of influence.

The second transition has been under way for at least a century, and it has its roots deep in the past. But it is far from complete today. In domestic politics authoritarianism is suspect; in child rearing we have made some wild swings, but exclusive reliance on authority is generally recognized today to create more problems than it solves; in religious organizations authority carries less force than it once did; husbands in our culture can no longer rely on authority to control the behavior of their wives.

A major difficulty is that we are not at all clear what we are trending *toward*. It is becoming evident after some trial-and-error learning that abdication is not an appropriate antithesis to authoritarianism, nor is there an answer in the simple compromise position halfway between the extremes. Only if we can free ourselves from the notion that we are limited to a single dimension—that of more or less authority—will we escape from our present dilemma. There are many alternatives to authority, not one. Each is appropriate for certain purposes and under certain conditions.

Authority is perfectly appropriate as a means of influencing behavior under certain circumstances. There is nothing inherently wrong or bad about giving an order or making a unilateral decision. There are many circumstances, however, when the exercise of authority fails to achieve the desired results. Under such circumstances, the solution does not lie in exerting more authority or less authority; *it lies in using other means of influence.*

If authority is the only tool in the manager's kit, he cannot hope to achieve his purposes very well, but it does not follow that he ought to throw away this tool. There are times when he will need it, when other tools will not be appropriate for his purposes.

The power to influence others is not a function of the amount of authority one can exert. It is, rather, a function of the appropriate selection of the means of influence which the particular circumstances require. Conventional organization theory teaches us that power and authority are coextensive. Consequently, relinquishing authority is seen as losing the power to control. This is a completely misleading conception.

We have today at least the basic knowledge to enable us to discriminate among several forms of influence and to recognize some of the conditions within which each is appropriate. That knowledge —limited though it is—has important implications for industral management.

REFERENCES

Argyris, Chris, *Personality and Organization.* New York: Harper & Brothers, 1957.

Bakke, E. Wight, *Bonds of Organization.* New York: Harper & Brothers, 1950. Yale Labor and Management Series.

Barnard, Chester I., *The Functions of the Executive.* Cambridge, Mass.: Harvard University Press, 1938.

Boulding, Kenneth E., *The Organizational Revolution.* New York: Harper & Brothers, 1953.

Drucker, Peter F., *The New Society.* New York: Harper & Brothers, 1950.

Drucker, Peter F., *The Practice of Management.* New York: Harper & Brothers, 1954.

Haire, Mason (ed.), *Modern Organization Theory.* New York: John Wiley & Sons, Jnc., 1959.

Harbison, Frederick, and Charles A. Myers, *Management in the Industrial World.* New York: McGraw-Hill Book Company, Inc., 1959.

Jacobson, E., W. W. Charters, Jr., and S. Lieberman, "The Use of the Role Concept in the Study of Complex Organizations," *Journal of Social Issues,* vol. 7, no. 3, 1951.

Metcalf, Henry C., and L. Urwick (eds.), *Dynamic Administration: The Collected Papers of Mary Parker Follett.* New York: Harper & Brothers, 1942.

Simon, Herbert A., *Administrative Behavior,* 2d ed., New York: The Macmillan Company, 1959.

Simon, Herbert A., "Authority," *Research in Industrial Human Relations.* New York: Harper & Brothers, 1957.

3

Theory X: The Traditional View
of Direction and Control

Behind every managerial decision or action are assumptions about human nature and human behavior. A few of these are remarkably pervasive. They are implicit in most of the literature of organization and in much current managerial policy and practice:

1. *The average human being has an inherent dislike of work and will avoid it if he can.*

This assumption has deep roots. The punishment of Adam and Eve for eating the fruit of the Tree of Knowledge was to be banished from Eden into a world where they had to work for a living. The stress that management places on productivity, on the concept of "a fair day's work," on the evils of featherbedding and restriction of output, on rewards for performance—while it has a logic in terms of the objectives of enterprise—reflects an underlying belief that management must counteract an inherent human

33

tendency to avoid work. The evidence for the correctness of this assumption would seem to most managers to be incontrovertible.

2. *Because of this human characteristic of dislike of work, most people must be coerced, controlled, directed, threatened with punishment to get them to put forth adequate effort toward the achievement of organizational objectives.*

The dislike of work is so strong that even the promise of rewards is not generally enough to overcome it. People will accept the rewards and demand continually higher ones, but these alone will not produce the necessary effort. Only the threat of punishment will do the trick.

The current wave of criticism of "human relations," the derogatory comments about "permissiveness" and "democracy" in industry, the trends in some companies toward recentralization after the postwar wave of decentralization—all these are assertions of the underlying assumption that people will only work under external coercion and control. The recession of 1957–1958 ended a decade of experimentation with the "soft" managerial approach, and this assumption (which never really was abandoned) is being openly espoused once more.

3. *The average human being prefers to be directed, wishes to avoid responsibility, has relatively little ambition, wants security above all.*

This assumption of the "mediocrity of the masses" is rarely expressed so bluntly. In fact, a good deal of lip service is given to the ideal of the worth of the average human being. Our political and social values demand such public expressions. Nevertheless, a great many managers will give private support to this assumption, and it is easy to see it reflected in policy and practice. Paternalism has become a nasty word, but it is by no means a defunct managerial philosophy.

I have suggested elsewhere the name Theory X for this set of assumptions. In later chapters of this book I will attempt to show that Theory X is not a straw man for purposes of demolition, but is in fact a theory which materially influences managerial strategy in a wide sector of American industry today. Moreover, the principles of organization which comprise the bulk of the literature of management *could only have been derived from assumptions such as those of Theory X*. Other beliefs about human nature would have led inevitably to quite different organizational principles.

Theory X provides an explanation of some human behavior in industry. These assumptions would not have persisted if there were not a considerable body of evidence to support them. Nevertheless, there are many readily observable phenomena in industry and elsewhere which are not consistent with this view of human nature.

Such a state of affairs is not uncommon. The history of science provides many examples of theoretical explanations which persist over long periods despite the fact that they are only partially adequate. Newton's laws of motion are a case in point. It was not until the development of the theory of relativity during the present century that important inconsistencies and inadequacies in Newtonian theory could be understood and corrected.

The growth of knowledge in the social sciences during the past quarter century has made it possible to reformulate some assumptions about human nature and human behavior in the organizational setting which resolve certain of the inconsistencies inherent in Theory X. While this reformulation is, of course, tentative, it provides an improved basis for prediction and control of human behavior in industry.

Some Assumptions about Motivation

At the core of any theory of the management of human resources are assumptions about human motivation. This has been a confusing subject because there have been so many conflicting points of view even among social scientists. In recent years, however, there has been a convergence of research findings and a growing acceptance of a few rather basic ideas about motivation. These ideas appear to have considerable power. They help to explain the inadequacies of Theory X as well as the limited sense in which it is correct. In addition, they provide the basis for an entirely different theory of management.

The following generalizations about motivation are somewhat oversimplified. If all of the qualifications which would be required by a truly adequate treatment were introduced, the gross essentials which are particularly significant for management would be obscured. These generalizations do not misrepresent the facts, but they do ignore some complexities of human behavior which are relatively unimportant for our purposes.

Man is a wanting animal—as soon as one of his needs is satisfied, another appears in its place. This process is unending. It continues from birth to death. Man continuously puts forth effort —works, if you please—to satisfy his needs.

Human needs are organized in a series of levels—a hierarchy of importance. At the lowest level, but preeminent in importance when they are thwarted, are the physiological needs. Man lives by bread alone, when there is no bread. Unless the circumstances are unusual, his needs for love, for status, for recognition are inoperative when his stomach has been empty for a while. But when he eats regularly and adequately, hunger ceases to be an important need. The sated man has hunger only in the sense that a full bottle has emptiness. The same is true of the other physiological needs of man—for rest, exercise, shelter, protection from the elements.

A satisfied need is not a motivator of behavior! This is a fact of profound significance. It is a fact which is unrecognized in Theory X and is, therefore, ignored in the conventional approach to the management of people. I shall return to it later. For the moment, an example will make the point. Consider your own need for air. Except as you are deprived of it, it has no appreciable motivating effect upon your behavior.

When the physiological needs are reasonably satisfied, needs at the next higher level begin to dominate man's behavior—to motivate him. These are the safety needs, for protection against danger, threat, deprivation. Some people mistakenly refer to these as needs for security. However, unless man is in a dependent relationship where he fears arbitrary deprivation, he does not demand security. The need is for the "fairest possible break." When he is confident of this, he is more than willing to take risks. But when he feels threatened or dependent, his greatest need is for protection, for security.

The fact needs little emphasis that since every industrial employee is in at least a partially dependent relationship, safety needs may assume considerable importance. Arbitrary management actions, behavior which arouses uncertainty with respect to continued employment or which reflects favoritism or discrimination, unpredictable administration of policy—these can be powerful motivators of the safety needs in the employment relationship at every level from worker to vice president. In addition, the safety needs of managers are often aroused by their dependence downward or laterally. This is a major reason for emphasis on management prerogatives and clear assignments of authority.

When man's physiological needs are satisfied and he is no longer fearful about his physical welfare, his social needs become important motivators of his behavior. These are such needs as those for belonging, for association, for acceptance by one's fellows, for giving and receiving friendship and love.

Management knows today of the existence of these needs, but it is often assumed quite wrongly that they represent a threat to the organization. Many studies have demonstrated that the tightly knit, cohesive work group may, under proper conditions, be far more effective than an equal number of separate individuals in achieving organizational goals. Yet management, fearing group hostility to its own objectives, often goes to considerable lengths to control and direct human efforts in ways that are inimical to the natural "groupiness" of human beings. When man's social needs—and perhaps his safety needs, too—are thus thwarted, he behaves in ways which tend to defeat organizational objectives. He becomes resistant, antagonistic, uncooperative. But this behavior is a consequence, not a cause.

Above the social needs—in the sense that they do not usually become motivators until lower needs are reasonably satisfied—are the needs of greatest significance to management and to man himself. They are the egoistic needs, and they are of two kinds:

1. Those that relate to one's self-esteem: needs for self-respect and self-confidence, for autonomy, for achievement, for competence, for knowledge
2. Those that relate to one's reputation: needs for status, for recognition, for appreciation, for the deserved respect of one's fellows

Unlike the lower needs, these are rarely satisfied; man seeks indefinitely for more satisfaction of these needs once they have become important to him. However, they do not usually appear in any significant way until physiological, safety, and social needs are reasonably satisfied. Exceptions to this generalization are to be observed, particularly under circumstances where, in addition to severe deprivation of physiological needs, human dignity is trampled upon. Political revolutions often grow out of thwarted social and ego, as well as physiological, needs.

The typical industrial organization offers only limited opportunities for the satisfaction of egoistic needs to people at lower levels in the hierarchy. The conventional methods of organizing work, particularly in mass production industries, give little heed to these aspects of human motivation. If the practices of "scientific management" were deliberately calculated to thwart these needs—

which, of course, they are not—they could hardly accomplish this purpose better than they do.

Finally—a capstone, as it were, on the hierarchy—there are the needs for self-fulfillment. These are the needs for realizing one's own potentialities, for continued self-development, for being creative in the broadest sense of that term.

The conditions of modern industrial life give only limited opportunity for these relatively dormant human needs to find expression. The deprivation most people experience with respect to other lower-level needs diverts their energies into the struggle to satisfy *those* needs, and the needs for self-fulfillment remain below the level of consciousness.

Now, briefly, a few general comments about motivation:

We recognize readily enough that a man suffering from a severe dietary deficiency is sick. The deprivation of physiological needs has behavioral consequences. The same is true, although less well recognized, of the deprivation of higher-level needs. The man whose needs for safety, association, independence, or status are thwarted is sick, just as surely as is he who has rickets. And his sickness will have behavioral consequences. We will be mistaken if we attribute his resultant passivity, or his hostility, or his refusal to accept responsibility to his inherent "human nature." These forms of behavior are *symptoms* of illness—of deprivation of his social and egoistic needs.

The man whose lower-level needs are satisfied is not motivated to satisfy *those* needs. For practical purposes they exist no longer. (Remember my point about your need for air.) Management often asks, "Why aren't people more productive? We pay good wages, provide good working conditions, have excellent fringe benefits and steady employment. Yet people do not seem to be willing to put forth more than minimum effort." It is unnecessary to look far for the reasons.

Consideration of the rewards typically provided the worker for satisfying his needs through his employment leads to the interesting conclusion that most of these rewards can be used for satisfying his needs *only when he leaves the job.* Wages, for example, cannot be spent at work. The only contribution they can make to his satisfaction on the job is in terms of status differences resulting from wage differentials. (This, incidentally, is one of the reasons why small and apparently unimportant differences in wage rates can be the subject of so much heated dispute. The issue is not the pennies involved, but the fact that the status differences which they reflect are one of the few ways in which wages can result in need satisfaction in the job situation itself.)

Most fringe benefits—overtime pay, shift differentials, vacations, health and medical benefits, annuities, and the proceeds from stock purchase plans or profit-sharing plans—yield needed satisfaction only when the individual leaves the job. Yet these, along with wages, are among the major rewards provided by management for effort. It is not surprising, therefore, that for many wage earners *work is perceived as a form of punishment* which is the price to be paid for various kinds of satisfaction away from the job. To the extent that this is their perception, we would hardly expect them to undergo more of this punishment than is necessary.

Under today's conditions management has provided relatively well for the satisfaction of physiological and safety needs. The standard of living in our country is high; people do not suffer major deprivation of their physiological needs except during periods of severe unemployment. Even then, the social legislation developed since the thirties cushions the shock.

But the fact that management has provided for these physiological and safety needs has shifted the motivational emphasis to the social and the egoistic needs. Unless there are opportunities *at work* to satisfy these higher-level needs, people will be deprived; and their behavior will reflect this deprivation. Under such conditions, if management continues to focus its attention on physiological needs, the mere provision of rewards is bound to be ineffective, and reliance on the threat of punishment will be inevitable. Thus one of the assumptions of Theory X will appear to be validated, but only because we have mistaken effects for causes.

People *will* make insistent demands for more money under these conditions. It becomes more important than ever to buy the material goods and services which can provide limited satisfaction of the thwarted needs. Although money has only limited value in satisfying many higher-level needs, it can become the focus of interest if it is the only means available.

The "carrot and stick" theory of motivation which goes along with Theory X works reasonably well under certain circumstances. The *means* for satisfying man's physiological and (within limits) safety needs can be provided or withheld by management. Employment itself is such a means, and so are wages, working conditions, and benefits. By these means the individual can be controlled so long as he is struggling for subsistence. Man tends to live for bread alone when there is little bread.

But the "carrot and stick" theory does not work at all once man has reached an adequate subsistence level and is motivated primarily by higher needs. Management cannot provide a man with self-respect, or with the respect of his fellows, or with the satisfaction of needs for self-fulfillment. We can create conditions such that he is encouraged and enabled to seek such satisfactions for himself, or we can thwart him by failing to create those conditions.

But this creation of conditions is not "control" in the usual sense; it does not seem to be a particularly good device for directing behavior. And so management finds itself in an odd position. The high standard of living created by our modern technological know-how provides quite adequately for the satisfaction of physiological and safety needs. The only significant exception is where management practices have not created confidence in a "fair break"—and thus where safety needs are thwarted. But by making possible the satisfaction of lower-level needs, management has deprived itself of the ability to use the control devices on which the conventional assumptions of Theory X has taught it to rely: rewards, promises, incentives, or threats and other coercive devices. The philosophy of management by direction and control— *regardless of whether it is hard or soft*—is inadequate to motivate because the human needs on which this approach relies are relatively unimportant motivators of behavior in our society today. Direction and control are of limited value in motivating people whose important needs are social and egoistic.

People, deprived of opportunities to satisfy at work the needs which are now important to them, behave exactly as we might predict—with indolence, passivity, unwillingness to accept responsibility, resistance to change, willingness to follow the demagogue, unreasonable demands for economic benefits. It would seem that we may be caught in a web of our own weaving.

Theory X explains the *consequences* of a particular managerial strategy; it neither explains nor describes human nature although it purports to. Because its assumptions are so unnecessarily limiting, it prevents our seeing the possibilities inherent in other managerial strategies. What sometimes appear to be new strategies— decentralization, management by objectives, consultative supervision, "democratic" leadership—are usually but old wine in new bottles because the procedures developed to implement them are derived from the same inadequate assumptions about human nature. Management is constantly becoming disillusioned with widely touted and expertly merchandized "new approaches" to the human side of enterprise. The real difficulty is that these new approaches are no more than different tactics—programs, procedures, gadgets—within an unchanged strategy based on Theory X.

In child rearing, it is recognized that parental strategies of control must be progressively modified to adapt to the changed capabilities and characteristics of the human individual as he develops from infancy to adulthood. To some extent industrial management recognizes that the human *adult* possesses capabilities for continued learning and growth. Witness the many current activities in the fields of training and management development. In its *basic* conceptions of managing human resources, however, management appears to have concluded that the average human being is permanently arrested in his development in early adolescence. Theory X is built on the least common human denominator: the factory "hand" of the past. As Chris Argyris has shown dramatically in his *Personality and Organization,* conventional managerial strategies for the organization, direction, and control of the human resources of enterprise are admirably suited to the capacities and characteristics of the child rather than the adult.

In one limited area—that of research administration—there has been some recent recognition of the need for selective adaptation in managerial strategy. This, however, has been perceived as a unique problem, and its broader implications have not been recognized. As pointed out in this and the previous chapter, changes in the population at large—in educational level, attitudes and values, motivation, degree of dependence—have created both the opportunity and the need for other forms of selective adaptation. However, so long as the assumptions of Theory X continue to influence managerial strategy, we will fail to discover, let alone utilize, the potentialities of the average human being.

REFERENCES

Allen, Louis A., *Management and Organization.* New York: McGraw-Hill Book Company, Inc., 1958.

Bendix, Reinhard, *Work and Authority in Industry.* New York: John Wiley & Sons, Inc., 1956.

Brown, Alvin, *Organization of Industry.* Englewood Cliffs, N.J.: Prentice-Hall, Inc., 1947.

Fayol, Henri, *General and Industrial Administration.* New York: Pitman Publishing Corporation, 1949.

Gouldner, Alvin W., *Patterns of Industrial Bureaucracy.* Glencoe, Ill.: Free Press, 1954.

Koontz, Harold, and Cyril O'Donnell, *Principles of Management*. New York: McGraw-Hill Book Company, Inc., 1955.

Maslow, A. H., *Motivation and Personality*. New York: Harper & Brothers, 1954.

Urwick, Lyndall, *The Elements of Administration*. New York: Harper & Brothers, 1944.

Walker, Charles R., *Toward the Automatic Factory*. New Haven, Conn.: Yale University Press, 1957.

Whyte, William F., *Money and Motivation*. New York: Harper & Brothers, 1955.

Zaleznik, A., C. R. Christensen, and F. J. Roethlisberger, *The Motivation, Productivity, and Satisfaction of Workers: A Prediction Study*. Boston: Division of Research, The Graduate School of Business Administration, Harvard University, 1958.

4

Theory Y: The Integration of Individual and Organizational Goals

To some, the preceding analysis will appear unduly harsh. Have we not made major modifications in the management of the human resources of industry during the past quarter century? Have we not recognized the importance of people and made vitally significant changes in managerial strategy as a consequence? Do the developments since the twenties in personnel administration and labor relations add up to nothing?

There is no question that important progress has been made in the past two or three decades. During this period the human side of enterprise has become a major preoccupation of management. A tremendous number of policies, programs, and practices which were virtually unknown thirty years ago have become commonplace. The lot of the industrial employee—be he worker, professional, or executive—has improved to a degree which could hardly have been imagined by his counterpart of the nineteen twenties. Management has adopted generally a far more humanitarian set of values; it has successfully striven to give more equitable and more generous treatment to its employees. It has significantly reduced economic hardships, eliminated the more extreme forms of industrial warfare, provided a generally safe and pleasant working environment, *but it has done all these things without changing its fundamental theory of management.* There are exceptions here and there, and they are important; nevertheless, the assumptions of Theory X remain predominant throughout our economy.

Management was subjected to severe pressures during the Great Depression of the thirties. The wave of public antagonism, the open warfare accompanying the unionization of the mass production industries, the general reaction against authoritarianism, the legislation of the New Deal produced a wide "pendulum swing." However, the changes in policy and practice which took place during that and the next decade were primarily adjustments to the increased power of organized labor and to the pressures of public opinion.

Some of the movement was away from "hard" and toward "soft" management, but it was short-lived, and for good reasons. It has become clear that many of the initial strategic interpretations accompanying the "human relations approach" were as naïve as those which characterized the early stages of progressive education. We have now discovered that there is no answer in the simple removal of control—that abdication is not a workable alternative to authoritarianism. We have learned that there is no direct correlation between employee satisfaction and productivity. We recognize today that "industrial democracy" cannot consist in permitting everyone to decide everything, that industrial health does not flow automatically from the elimination of dissatisfaction, disagreement, or even open conflict. Peace is not synonymous with organizational health; socially responsible management is not co-extensive with permissive management.

Now that management has regained its earlier prestige and power, it has become obvious that the trend toward "soft" management was a temporary and relatively superficial reaction rather than a general modification of fundamental assumptions or basic strategy. Moreover, while the progress we have made in the past quarter century is substantial, it has reached the point of diminishing returns. The tactical possibilities within conventional managerial strategies have been pretty completely exploited, and significant new developments will be unlikely without major modifications in theory.

The Assumptions of Theory Y

There have been few dramatic break-throughs in social science theory like those which have occurred in the physical sciences during the past half century. Nevertheless, the accumulation of knowledge about human behavior in many specialized fields has made possible the formulation of a number of generalizations which provide a modest beginning for new theory with respect to the management of human resources. Some of these assumptions were outlined in the discussion of motivation in Chapter 3. Some others, which will hereafter be referred to as Theory Y, are as follows:

1. *The expenditure of physical and mental effort in work is as natural as play or rest.* The average human being does not inherently dislike work. Depending upon controllable conditions, work may be a source of satisfaction (and will be voluntarily performed) or a source of punishment (and will be avoided if possible).

2. *External control and the threat of punishment are not the only means for bringing about effort toward organizational objectives. Man will exercise self-direction and self-control in the service of objectives to which he is committed.*

3. *Commitment to objectives is a function of the rewards associated with their achievement.* The most significant of such rewards, e.g., the satisfaction of ego and self-actu-

alization needs, can be direct products of effort directed toward organizational objectives.

4. *The average human being learns, under proper conditions, not only to accept but to seek responsibility.* Avoidance of responsibility, lack of ambition, and emphasis on security are generally consequences of experience, not inherent human characteristics.

5. *The capacity to exercise a relatively high degree of imagination, ingenuity, and creativity in the solution of organizational problems is widely, not narrowly, distributed in the population.*

6. *Under the conditions of modern industrial life, the intellectual potentialities of the average human being are only partially utilized.*

These assumptions involve sharply different implications for managerial strategy than do those of Theory X. They are dynamic rather than static: They indicate the possibility of human growth and development; they stress the necessity for selective adaptation rather than for a single absolute form of control. They are not framed in terms of the least common denominator of the factory hand, but in terms of a resource which has substantial potentialities.

Above all, the assumptions of Theory Y point up the fact that the limits on human collaboration in the organizational setting are not limits of human nature but of management's ingenuity in discovering how to realize the potential represented by its human resources. Theory X offers management an easy rationalization for ineffective organizational performance: It is due to the nature of the human resources with which we must work. Theory Y, on the other hand, places the problems squarely in the lap of management. If employees are lazy, indifferent, unwilling to take responsibility, intransigent, uncreative, uncooperative, Theory Y implies that the causes lie in management's methods of organization and control.

The assumptions of Theory Y are not finally validated. Nevertheless, they are far more consistent with existing knowledge in the social sciences than are the assumptions of Theory X. They will undoubtedly be refined, elaborated, modified as further research accumulates, but they are unlikely to be completely contradicted.

On the surface, these assumptions may not seem particularly difficult to accept. Carrying their implications into practice, however, is not easy. They challenge a number of deeply ingrained managerial habits of thought and action.

The Principle of Integration

The central principle of organization which derives from Theory X is that of direction and control through the exercise of authority —what has been called "the scalar principle." The central principle which derives from Theory Y is that of integration: the creation of conditions such that the members of the organization can achieve their own goals *best* by directing their efforts toward the success of the enterprise. These two principles have profoundly different implications with respect to the task of managing human resources, but the scalar principle is so firmly built into managerial attitudes that the implications of the principle of integration are not easy to perceive.

Someone once said that fish discover water last. The "psychological environment" of industrial management—like water for fish —is so much a part of organizational life that we are unaware of it. Certain characteristics of our society, and of organizational life within it, are so completely established, so pervasive, that we cannot conceive of their being otherwise. As a result, a great many policies and practices and decisions and relationships could only be—it seems—what they are.

Among these pervasive characteristics of organizational life in the United States today is a managerial attitude (stemming from

Theory X) toward membership in the industrial organization. It is assumed almost without question that organizational requirements take precedence over the needs of individual members. Basically, the employment agreement is that in return for the rewards which are offered, the individual will accept external direction and control. The very idea of integration and self-control is foreign to our way of thinking about the employment relationship. The tendency, therefore, is either to reject it out of hand (as socialistic, or anarchistic, or inconsistent with human nature) or to twist it unconsciously until it fits existing conceptions.

The concept of integration and self-control carries the implication that the organization will be more effective in achieving its economic objectives if adjustments are made, in significant ways, to the needs and goals of its members.

A district manager in a large, geographically decentralized company is notified that he is being promoted to a policy level position at headquarters. It is a big promotion with a large salary increase. His role in the organization will be a much more powerful one, and he will be associated with the major executives of the firm.

The headquarters group who selected him for this position have carefully considered a number of possible candidates. This man stands out among them in a way which makes him the natural choice. His performance has been under observation for some time, and there is little question that he possesses the necessary qualifications, not only for this opening but for an even higher position. There is genuine satisfaction that such an outstanding candidate is available.

The man is appalled. He doesn't want the job. His goal, as he expresses it, is to be the "best damned district manager in the company." He enjoys his direct associations with operating people in the field, and he doesn't want a policy level job. He and his wife enjoy the kind of life they have created in a small city, and they dislike actively both the living conditions and the social obligations of the headquarters city. He expresses his feelings as strongly as he can, but his objections are brushed aside. The organization's needs are such that his refusal to accept the promotion would be unthinkable. His superiors say to themselves that of course when he has settled in to the new job, he will recognize that it was the right thing. And so he makes the move.

Two years later he is in an even higher position in the company's headquarters organization, and there is talk that he will probably be the executive vice-president before long. Privately he expresses considerable unhappiness and dissatisfaction. He (and his wife) would "give anything" to be back in the situation he left two years ago.

Within the context of the pervasive assumptions of Theory X, promotions and transfers in large numbers are made by unilateral decision. The requirements of the organization are given priority automatically and almost without question. If the individual's personal goals are considered at all, it is assumed that the rewards of salary and position will satisfy him. Should an individual actually refuse such a move without a compelling reason, such as health or a severe family crisis, he would be considered to have jeopardized his future because of this "selfish" attitude. It is rare indeed for management to give the individual the opportunity to be a genuine and active partner in such a decision, even though it may affect his most important personal goals. Yet the implications following from Theory Y are that the organization is likely to suffer if it ignores these personal needs and goals. In making unilateral decisions with respect to promotion, management is failing to utilize its human resources in the most effective way.

The principle of integration demands that both the organization's and the individual's needs be recognized. Of course, when there is a sincere joint effort to find it, an integrative solution which meets the needs of the individual *and* the organization is a frequent outcome. But not always—and this is the point at which Theory Y begins to appear unrealistic. It collides head on with pervasive attitudes associated with management by direction and control.

The assumptions of Theory Y imply that unless integration is achieved *the organization will suffer*. The objectives of the organization are *not* achieved best by the unilateral administration of promotions, because this form of management by direction and control will not create the commitment which would make available the full resources of those affected. The lesser motivation, the lesser resulting degree of self-direction and self-control are costs which, when added up for many instances over time, will more than offset the gains obtained by unilateral decisions "for the good of the organization."

One other example will perhaps clarify further the sharply different implications of Theory X and Theory Y.

It could be argued that management is already giving a great deal of attention to the principle of integration through its efforts in the field of economic education. Many millions of dollars and much ingenuity have been expended in attempts to persuade employees that their welfare is intimately connected with the success of the free enterprise system and of their own companies. The idea that they can achieve their own goals best by directing their effort toward the objectives of the organization has been explored and developed and communicated in every possible way. Is this not evidence that management is already committed to the principle of integration?

The answer is a definite no. These managerial efforts, with rare exceptions, reflect clearly the influence of the assumptions of Theory X. The central message is an exhortation to the industrial employee to work hard and follow orders in order to protect his job and his standard of living. Much has been achieved, it says, by our established way of running industry, and much more could be achieved if employees would adapt themselves *to management's definition* of what is required. Behind these exhortations lies the expectation that of course the requirements of the organization and its economic success must have priority over the needs of the individual.

Naturally, integration means working together for the success of the enterprise so we all may share in the resulting rewards. But management's implicit assumption is that working together means adjusting to the requirements of the organization *as management perceives them.* In terms of existing views, it seems inconceivable that individuals, seeking their own goals, would further the ends of the enterprise. On the contrary, this would lead to anarchy, chaos, irreconcilable conflicts of self-interest, lack of responsibility, inability to make decisions, and failure to carry out those that were made.

All these consequences, and other worse ones, *would* be inevitable unless conditions could be created such that the members of the organization perceived that they could achieve their own goals *best* by directing their efforts toward the success of the enterprise. If the assumptions of Theory Y are valid, the practical question is whether, and to what extent, such conditions can be created. To that question the balance of this volume is addressed.

The Application of Theory Y

In the physical sciences there are many theoretical phenomena which cannot be achieved in practice. Absolute zero and a perfect vacuum are examples. Others, such as nuclear power, jet aircraft, and human space flight, are recognized theoretically to be possible long before they become feasible. This fact does not make theory less useful. If it were not for our theoretical convictions, we would not even be attempting to develop the means for human flight into space today. In fact, were it not for the development of physical science theory during the past century and a half, we would still be depending upon the horse and buggy and the sailing vessel for transportation. Virtually all significant technological developments wait on the formulation of relevant theory.

Similarly, in the management of the human resources of industry, the assumptions and theories about human nature at any given time limit innovation. Possibilities are not recognized, innovating efforts are not undertaken, until theoretical conceptions lay a groundwork for them. Assumptions like those of Theory X permit us to conceive of certain possible ways of organizing and directing human effort, *but not others*. Assumptions like those of Theory Y open up a range of possibilities for new managerial policies and practices. As in the case of the development of new physical science theory, some of these possibilities are not immediately feasible, and others may forever remain unattainable. They may be too costly, or it may be that we simply cannot discover how to create the necessary "hardware."

There is substantial evidence for the statement that the potentialities of the average human being are far above those which we typically realize in industry today. If our assumptions are like those of Theory X, we will not even recognize the existence of these potentialities and there will be no reason to devote time, effort, or money to discovering how to realize them. If, however, we accept assumptions like those of Theory Y, we will be challenged to innovate, to discover new ways of organizing and directing human effort, even though we recognize that the perfect organization, like the perfect vacuum, is practically out of reach.

We need not be overwhelmed by the dimensions of the managerial task implied by Theory Y. To be sure, a large mass production operation in which the workers have been organized by a militant and hostile union faces management with problems which appear at present to be insurmountable with respect to the application of the principle of integration. It may be decades before sufficient knowledge will have accumulated to make such an application feasible. Applications of Theory Y will have to be tested initially in more limited ways and under more favorable circumstances. However, a number of applications of Theory Y *in managing managers and professional people* are possible today. Within the managerial hierarchy, the assumptions can be tested and refined, techniques can be invented and skill acquired in their use. As knowledge accumulates, some of the problems of application at the worker level in large organizations may appear less baffling than they do at present.

Perfect integration of organizational requirements and individual goals and needs is, of course, not a realistic objective. In adopting this principle, we seek that degree of integration in which the individual can achieve his goals *best* by directing his efforts toward the success of the organization. "Best" means that this alternative will be more attractive than the many others available to him: indifference, irresponsibility, minimal compliance, hostility, sabotage. It means that he will continuously be encouraged to develop and utilize voluntarily his capacities, his knowledge, his skill, his ingenuity in ways which contribute to the success of the enterprise.[1]

---

[1] A recent, highly significant study of the sources of job satisfaction and dissatisfaction among managerial and professional people suggests that these opportunities for "self-actualization" are the essential requirements of both job satisfaction and high performance. The researchers find that "the wants of employees divide into two groups. One group revolves around the need to develop in one's occupation as a source of personal growth. The second group operates as an essential base to the first and is associated with fair treatment in compensation, supervision, working conditions, and administrative practices. *The fulfillment of the needs of the second group does not motivate the individual to high levels of job satisfaction and . . . to extra performance on the job.* All we can expect from satisfying [this second group of needs] is the prevention of dissatisfaction and poor job performance." Frederick Herzberg, Bernard Mausner, and Barbara Bloch Snyderman, *The Motivation to Work*. New York: John Wiley & Sons, Inc., 1959, pp. 114–115. (Italics mine.)

Acceptance of Theory Y does not imply abdication, or "soft" management, or "permissiveness." As was indicated above, such notions stem from the acceptance of authority as the *single* means of managerial control, and from attempts to minimize its negative consequences. Theory Y assumes that people will exercise self-direction and self-control in the achievement of organizational objectives *to the degree that they are committed to those objectives.* If that commitment is small, only a slight degree of self-direction and self-control will be likely, and a substantial amount of external influence will be necessary. If it is large, many conventional external controls will be relatively superfluous, and to some extent self-defeating. Managerial policies and practices materially affect this degree of commitment.

Authority is an inappropriate means for obtaining commitment to objectives. Other forms of influence—help in achieving integration, for example—are required for this purpose. Theory Y points to the possibility of lessening the emphasis on external forms of control to the degree that commitment to organizational objectives can be achieved. Its underlying assumptions emphasize the capacity of human beings for self-control, and the consequent possibility of greater managerial reliance on other means of influence. Nevertheless, it is clear that authority *is* an appropriate means for control under certain circumstances—particularly where genuine commitment to objectives cannot be achieved. The assumptions of Theory Y do not deny the appropriateness of authority, but they do deny that it is appropriate for all purposes and under all circumstances.

Many statements have been made to the effect that we have acquired today the know-how to cope with virtually any technological problems which may arise, and that the major industrial advances of the next half century will occur on the human side of enterprise. Such advances, however, are improbable so long as management continues to organize and direct and control its human resources on the basis of assumptions—tacit or explicit—like those of Theory X. Genuine innovation, in contrast to a refurbishing and patching of present managerial strategies, requires first the acceptance of less limiting assumptions about the nature of the human resources we seek to control, and second the readiness to adapt selectively to the implications contained in those new assumptions. Theory Y is an invitation to innovation.

REFERENCES

Brown, J. A. C., *The Social Psychology of Industry*. Baltimore: Penguin Books, Inc., 1954.

Cordiner, Ralph J., *New Frontiers for Professional Managers*. New York: McGraw-Hill Book Company, Inc., 1956.

Dubin, Robert, *The World of Work: Industrial Society and Human Relations*. Englewood Cliffs, N.J.: Prentice-Hall, Inc., 1958.

Friedmann, Georges, *Industrial Society: The Emergence of the Human Problems of Automation*. Glencoe, Ill.: Free Press, 1955.

Herzberg, Freaerick, Bernard Mausner, and Barbara Bloch Snyderman, *The Motivation to Work*. New York: John Wiley & Sons, Inc., 1959.

Krech, David, and Richard S. Crutchfield, *Theory and Problems of Social Psychology*. New York: McGraw-Hill Book Company, Inc., 1948.

Leavitt, Harold J., *Managerial Psychology*. Chicago: University of Chicago Press, 1958.

McMurry, Robert N., "The Case for Benevolent Autocracy," *Harvard Business Review*, vol. 36, no. 1 (January–February), 1958.

Rice, A. K., *Productivity and Social Organizations: The Ahmedabad Experiment*. London: Tavistock Publications, Ltd., 1958.

Stagner, Ross, *The Psychology of Industrial Conflict*. New York: John Wiley & Sons, Inc., 1956.

PART TWO: THEORY Y IN PRACTICE

5

Management by Integration
and Self-control

Let us now consider in some detail a specific illustration of the
operation of a managerial strategy based on Theory Y. The concept of "management by objectives" has received considerable attention in recent years, in part due to the writings of Peter Drucker.
However, management by objectives has often been interpreted in
a way which leads to no more than a new set of tactics within a
strategy of management by direction and control.

The strategy to be illustrated in the following pages is an application of Theory Y. Its purpose is to encourage integration, to
create a situation in which a subordinate can achieve his own goals
best by directing his efforts toward the objectives of the enterprise.
It is a deliberate attempt to link improvement in managerial competence with the satisfaction of higher-level ego and self-actualization needs. It is thus a special and not at all a typical case of the
conventional conception of management by objectives.

This strategy includes four steps or phases:

1. The clarification of the broad requirements of the job
2. The establishment of specific "targets" for a limited time period
3. The management process during the target period
4. Appraisal of the results

Harry Evans is Vice President, Staff Services, for a manufacturing company with twenty plants throughout the Middle West and the South. The company is aggressively managed and financially successful; it is growing fairly rapidly through acquisition of smaller companies and the development of new markets for its products.

Evans was brought into the company three years ago by the President, who felt that the staff functions of the organization needed strengthening. One of the President's concerns was the personnel department, which had been something of a stepchild since it was established in the early forties. He felt that the management needed a lot of help and guidance in order to fulfill its responsibilities in this field.

Tom Harrison has been Director of Personnel Administration for a little less than a year. Evans selected him from among a number of candidates. Although he is not as well trained professionally as some of his colleagues, he appeared to have good promise as an administrator. He is in his young forties, intelligent, ambitious, personable, a hard worker with ten years of practical experience in personnel administration.

After Harrison had been on the job a few months, Evans had formed the following impressions about him:

1. He is overly anxious to make a good impression on top management, and this interferes with his performance. He watches too carefully to see which way the wind is blowing and trims his sails accordingly. He accepts even the most trivial assignments from any of the top management group, which makes a good im-

pression but does little to strengthen the personnel function. He has done nothing to change the rather naïve top management expectation that personnel administration can be delegated to a staff department ("You take care of the personnel problems and we'll run the business.").

2. Harrison is a poor manager, somewhat to Evans's surprise, since he appeared to function well with more limited supervisory responsibilities. He uses his subordinates as errand boys rather than as resources, and he is much too ready to impose upon them his own practical and common-sense views of what should be done, brushing aside their specialized professional knowledge. He is anxious to reorganize the department, giving key responsibilities to men like himself who have practical experience but limited professional training.

These things added up, in Evans's eyes, to an inadequate conception of the nature of the personnel job and the proper role of the department within the company. He recognized the value of management's acceptance of Harrison's practical orientation, but he felt that the real needs of the company would not be met unless management acquired a quite different point of view with respect to the function. He was not at all inclined to replace Harrison, since he believed he had the capacity to perform effectively, but he recognized that Harrison was not going to grow into the job without help. His strategy involved the four steps listed below.

Step 1. *Determining the Major Requirements of the Job.* Evans suggested to Harrison that he would like him to give some intensive thought to the nature of his job in the light of his experience so far. He asked him to list what he felt to be his major responsibilities, using the formal position description in his possession if he wished, but not limiting himself to it. He said, "I'd like to discuss with you at some length *your* view of your job after being on it for the past eight months."

The list of requirements which Harrison subsequently brought in for discussion with Evans was as follows:

1. Organization of the Department
2. Services to top management
   a. Awareness of company problems and provision of programs and policies for solving them
3. Productivity of the Department
   a. Efficient administration of personnel programs and services
   b. Definite assignments of projects to staff with completion dates and follow-up
   c. Periodic appraisals of the performance of department members, with appropriate action
4. Field relations
   a. Providing the field units with advice, adequate programs, information
   b. Periodic visits to assure the adequacy of field personnel units

Harrison and Evans had several lengthy discussions of this list of responsibilities. Evans began by saying, "Tom, I asked you to bring to this meeting a written statement of the major requirements of your job as you see them. Perhaps you expected me to define your job for you, to tell you what I want you to do. If I were to do so, it would not be your job. Of course, I don't expect that I will necessarily see eye to eye with you on everything you have written down. I do take it for granted that we have a common purpose: We both want yours to be the best damned personnel department anywhere.

"The difficulty we are likely to have in discussing your ideas is that if I disagree with you, you'll feel you have to accept what I say because I'm your boss. I want to help you end up with a list that we are both completely satisfied with, but I can't help if you simply defer to my ideas or if I don't express them for fear of dominating you. So try to think of me as a colleague whose experience and knowledge are at your disposal—not as your boss. I'm certain we can resolve any differences that may come up."

In the course of the discussion Evans did bring up his concerns, but he put major emphasis on encouraging Harrison to examine his own ideas critically. Evans talked quite frankly about the realities of the company situation as he saw them, and he discussed his conception of the proper role for a personnel department. He tried to persuade Harrison that his conception of the personnel function was too limited, and that his own subordinates, because of their training and experience, could help him arrive at a more adequate conception. Harrison held a couple of meetings with his own department staff to discuss this whole question, and after each of them he had further conversations with Evans.

The critically significant factor in these discussions was not their content, but the redefinition of roles which took place. Evans succeeded, by his manner more than by his specific words, in conveying to Harrison the essential point that he did not want to occupy the conventional role of boss, but rather, to the fullest extent possible, the role of a consultant who was putting all of his knowledge and experience at Harrison's disposal in the conviction that they had a genuine common interest in Harrison's doing an outstanding job.

As he began to sense this, and to believe it, Harrison's whole perception of his own role changed. Instead of seeking to find out, as would be natural under conventional circumstances, how Evans wanted him to define his job, what Evans wanted him to do, what Evans would approve or disapprove, Harrison began to think for himself. Moreover, with this greater sense of freedom about his own role (and with Evans's open encouragement) he began to perceive his own subordinates not as "hands," but as resources, and to use them thus.

The result, unrealistic as it may seem at first glance, was a dramatic change in Harrison's perception of himself and of his job. The true nature of the change that took place during these discussions with Evans and with his subordinates was revealed in his final statement of his responsibilities as he now perceived them:

1. Organization of the Department
2. Continuous assessment of both short- and long-run company needs through:
   a. Exploration in the field
   b. General awareness of management's problems
   c. Exploration of the views of members of the Department
   d. Knowledge of external trends
3. Professional help to all levels of management
   a. Problem solving
   b. Strategy planning
   c. Research studies
   d. Effective personnel programs and policies
   e. Efficient administration of services
4. Development of staff members
5. Personal development

This first step in Evans's managerial strategy with Harrison is thus consistent with his commitment to Theory Y. He believes that Harrison must take the major responsibility for his own development, but he believes he can help. He conceives of integration as an active process which inevitably involves differences of opinion and argument. He recognizes the likelihood that Harrison may accede too readily to his views without real conviction, and he does not want this to happen. Consequently he attempts to establish a relationship in which Harrison can perceive him as a genuine source of help rather than as a boss in the conventional sense. He knows that the establishment of this relationship will take time, but it is the long-term results which he considers important. Since he does not expect that Harrison will grow into his job overnight, he is prepared to accept a definition of Harrison's job which is considerably short of perfection. He is confident that it will be improved six months hence when they discuss it again.

If Harrison is going to learn and grow in competence, and if he is going to find opportunities to satisfy his higher-level needs in the process, it is essential that he find a genuine challenge in his job. This is unlikely if the job is defined for him by a formal position description or by a superior who simply tells him what he wants done. Thus, the principle of integration is important right at the start. It is not necessary in applying it to ignore the work of the organization planning staff. The necessity for a logical division of responsibilities within any organization is obvious. However, a position description is likely to become a strait jacket unless it is recognized to be a broad set of guidelines within which the individual literally makes his own job. The conception of an organization plan as a series of predetermined "slots" into which individuals are selectively placed denies the whole idea of integration.

The process involved at this step is similar, although more limited in scope, to the one so aptly described by Drucker as discovering "what business we are in." In the case of top management looking at the organization as a whole, this frequently is a highly instructive experience. The same thing can be true even in a limited setting such as this, especially if the superior can, by doing something like Evans is doing, encourage the subordinate to think creatively about his job.

Step 2. Setting Targets. When Evans and Harrison finished their discussion of the major requirements of Harrison's job, Evans suggested that Harrison think about some specific objectives or targets which he might set for himself and his department during the following six months. Evans suggested that he think both about improving the over-all performance of his unit and about his own personal goals. He asked him further to consider in broad terms what steps he proposed to take to achieve these targets. Evans said, "I don't want to tell you how to do your job, but I would like you to do some careful thinking about how you are going to proceed. Perhaps I can be helpful when we discuss your ideas." Finally, Evans asked Harrison to consider what information he would require, and how he might obtain it, in order to know at the end of the period how well he had succeeded in reaching his targets. He suggested that they get together to talk further when Harrison had completed his thinking and planning along these lines.

This is the planning phase, but again the process is one in which the subordinate is encouraged to take responsibility for his own performance. The conventional process is one in which objectives are conceived by higher levels and imposed on lower levels of the organization. The rationale is that only the higher levels have available the broader knowledge necessary for planning. To some extent this is true, but there is an important difference between the kind of planning in which a central group determines in detail what each division or department will do, and that in which the central group communicates what are believed to be the desirable over-all objectives and *asks* each unit to determine what it can contribute.

Even when general objectives are predetermined, they can usually be limited to certain aspects of performance such as production goals, costs, and profit margin. There are other aspects which are subject to local determination, as is, of course, the planning with respect to personal objectives.

The important theoretical consideration, derived from Theory Y, is that the acceptance of responsibility (for self-direction and self-control) is correlated with commitment to objectives. Genuine commitment is seldom achieved when objectives are externally imposed. Passive acceptance is the most that can be expected; indifference or resistance are the more likely consequences. Some degree of *mutual* involvement in the determination of objectives is a necessary aspect of managerial planning based on Theory Y. This is embodied in Evans's suggestions to Harrison.

In the discussion of targets, the superior again attempts a helping role rather than an authoritative one. His primary interest is in helping the subordinate plan his own job in such a fashion that both personal and organizational goals will be achieved. While the superior has a veto power by virtue of his position, he will exercise it only if it becomes absolutely necessary.

To be sure, subordinates will sometimes set unrealistic goals, particularly the first time they approach a task like this. Experience has indicated that the usual problem is that the goals are set too high, not too low. While the superior can, through judicious advice, help the subordinate adjust unrealistic goals, there may often be greater long-run advantages in permitting the subordinate to learn by experience than in simply telling him where his planning is unrealistic or inadequate.

The list of targets which Harrison brought for discussion with Evans was this:

1. Determination of major company needs, long and short range, by:
   a. Field visits and discussions with local management
   b. Intensive discussions with top management
   c. Exploration of the views of the personnel department staff
   A plan, with assignments of responsibility, and a time schedule will be worked out for this. I expect we can complete the study within six months, but a report and subsequent plans will probably not be completed by September.
2. Joint determination with department staff of current projects
   This will involve planning such as you and I are doing.
3. Development of departmental staff members
   Items 1 and 2 can be a vehicle for this. I need help in learning how to work better with my subordinates, and particularly on how to eliminate the friction between the old-timers and the college-trained youngsters.

4. Self-development
   a. I'd like to do some reading to improve my own think-
      ing about personnel administration—or maybe take a
      university course. I'd like your advice.
   b. I guess I haven't gained as much skill as a manager as
      I need. I hear rumblings that some of my staff are not
      happy with me as a boss. I'd like to do something
      about this, but I'm not sure what is the best way to
      proceed.
5. Development of a good plan of organization for the department
   In working through some of the above projects, I think
   I'll get some good ideas about how we ought to be set
   up as a department.

Since the working relationship between the two men had been
quite well established during their earlier discussions, there was a
comfortable give and take at this stage. Evans saw the first target
as a crucial one which could become the basis for an entirely new
conception of the department's role. He felt also that it could be
extremely educational for Harrison provided he tackled it with
sensitivity and an open mind. Accordingly he spent several hours
helping Harrison to think through his strategy for determining
the needs of the company with respect to personnel administration. Harrison began to see that this project was a means by
which he could work toward all the other targets on his list.

Evans had little difficulty after Harrison's earlier experiences in
persuading him to involve his subordinates in developing plans
for the project. He suggested that Harrison continue to meet with
him to discuss and evaluate this process for a couple of months.
He felt—and said—that this might be the best method for Harrison to begin improving his own managerial skills.

They agreed that Harrison would explore possible university
programs during the next few months to see if some one of these
might meet his needs a little later. Meanwhile, they worked out a

reading list and a plan for an occasional session when Harrison could discuss his reading.

In view of the nature of the personnel function, and the particular problems facing Harrison, the targets did not lend themselves to quantitative measurement such as might have been possible in a production operation. Nevertheless, Harrison, under Evans's tutelage, worked out a fairly detailed plan with specific steps to be accomplished by the end of six months. Evans's interest was that Harrison would have a basis for evaluating his own accomplishments at the end of the period.

Evans brought into the discussion the question of their relationship during the ensuing period. He said, "I don't want to be in a position of checking up on you from week to week. These are your plans, and I have full confidence that you will make every effort to reach your targets. On the other hand, I want you to feel free to seek help if you want it. There are ways in which I believe my experience can be useful to you. Suppose we leave it that we'll get together on your initiative as often as you wish—not for you to report how you are doing, but to discuss any problems which you would like my help on, or any major revisions in your plans." Thus Evans helped Harrison still further to perceive the role that he wanted to occupy as a superior, and thus also to clarify his own responsibilities as a subordinate.

Step 3. The Ensuing Period. Since this is a managerial strategy rather than a personnel technique, the period between the establishment of targets and the evaluation of accomplishment is just as important as the first two steps. What happens during this period will depend upon the unique circumstances. The aim is to further the growth of the subordinate: his increased competence, his full acceptance of responsibility (self-direction and self-control), his ability to achieve integration between organizational requirements and his own personal goals.

In this particular situation Evans's primary interests were two: (1) the emergence throughout the company of a more adequate conception of the personnel function, and (2) the development of a competent department which would provide leadership and professional help to all levels of management with respect to this function. He felt that, as a result of steps 1 and 2 of his strategy, Harrison too was committed to these objectives. Moreover, he was persuaded that Harrison's project for assessing company needs in the field of personnel administration—as now conceived—was a highly promising means to these ends. He warned himself that he must be careful on two counts. First he must not expect too much too fast. The company situation was in no sense critical and there was no need for a crash program. Harrison's project was certain to be a valuable learning experience for him and his staff.

Second, Evans recognized that if the best learning was to occur, he must curb his natural tendency to step in and guide the project. Harrison would make mistakes; at his present level of sophistication he would quite possibly fail to appreciate the full scope of the task. Nevertheless, Evans decided more would be gained if he limited his influence to those occasions when Harrison sought his help.

This is what he did. His confidence in Harrison proved to have been justified. He and his staff tackled the project with more ingenuity and sensitivity than Evans would have imagined possible and began rather quickly to understand the true dimensions of the problem. Harrison came in one day to tell him that they had decided to extend their explorations to include visits to several university centers in order to take advantage of the point of view of some top-flight academic people. Also, they planned to test some of their emerging ideas against the experience of several other companies.

After this discussion, and the evidence it provided concerning the expansion of Harrison's intellectual horizons and the use he was making of the resources represented by his subordinates, Evans stopped worrying. He would bail them out if they got into trouble, but he anticipated no such necessity.

Step 4. *Self-appraisal.* At the end of August, Harrison reminded Evans (not vice versa!) that the six months was up. "When do you want a report?" was his question. Evans responded that a report was not what he wanted, but Harrison's own evaluation of what he had accomplished with respect to the targets he had set six months earlier. Said Evans, "This can give you a basis for planning for the next six months."

A week later Harrison brought the following notes to a discussion with Evans.

Appraisal, September 1

1. Determination of major company needs:
   a. The field work is completed.
   b. My staff and I are working on a proposal that will involve a new conception of personnel administration in this company. We will have a draft for discussion with you within thirty days, and we want you to take a full day to let us present our findings and proposals to you.
   c. The results of our work make it clear that we have an educational job to do with top management, and I want to include a plan along these lines in my next set of targets.
2. Joint determination with staff of current projects. I am now conducting a set of target-setting meetings with my department staff as a whole in which we are laying our plans for the next year. All major projects—individual or group—are being discussed out in detail there. These department meetings will be followed by individual planning sessions.
3. Development of department staff members
   a. The major project we have been carrying out has changed my ideas about several of my subordinates. I'm learning how to work with them, and it's clear they

are growing. Our presentation to you next month will show you what I mean.

   b. I've appreciated how much your target-setting approach has helped my development, and I'm attempting to use it with each of my subordinates. Also, I think the departmental planning mentioned under 2 above is a developmental tool. I've been talking with some people in the B_____ Company who do this and I'm excited about its possibilities in our own company.

4. Self-development
   All I can say is I've learned more in the past six months than in the previous five years.

5. Departmental organization
   I haven't done a thing about it. It doesn't seem very important right now. We seem to be able to plan our work as a department pretty well without developing a new setup. Perhaps we'll need to come back to this during the next six months, but there are more important things to be done first.

6. General comment
   I would rate myself considerably lower than I would have six months ago in terms of how well I'm filling the responsibilities of my job. It's going to take me a couple of years to measure up to what you have a right to expect of the man in this spot, but I think I can do it.

The discussion of this self-appraisal went into considerable detail. Evans felt that Harrison had acquired quite a little insight into his own strengths and weaknesses, and they were able to discuss objectively where he needed to give thought to improving his competence further. Harrison, for example, opened up the whole problem of his "yes-man" attitude in dealing with top management and pointed out that his exploratory interviews with some of these men had resulted in increased self-confidence. He said, "I think maybe I can learn to stand up for my ideas better in the future. You have helped me to realize that I can think for myself, and that I can defend myself in an argument."

They agreed to postpone Harrison's discussion of plans for the next six months until after the one-day session at which Evans would meet with the whole department. "Then," said Harrison, "I want to talk over with you a new statement of my responsibilities which I'm working on."

Managerial Strategy versus Personnel Techniques

The most important point with respect to management by integration and self-control is that it is a strategy—a way of managing people. The tactics are worked out in the light of the circumstances. Forms and procedures are of relatively little value. I stress this point because it has been my frequent experience, ever since some of my colleagues and I began to talk publicly about target setting, to have people send or bring me *forms* (often with the heading "self-appraisal") with the request that I tell them whether "this is all right" as a means of installing a new program.

"Selling" management a program of target setting, and providing standardized forms and procedures, is the surest way to *prevent* the development of management by integration and self-control. The manager who finds the underlying assumptions of Theory Y congenial will invent his own tactics provided he has a conception of the strategy involved. The manager whose underlying assumptions are those of Theory X cannot manage by integration and self-control no matter what techniques or forms are provided him.

If a staff department is interested in the potential values of target setting, the approach will be to devise means of getting management to examine its assumptions, to consider the consequences of its present strategy and to compare it with others. The tools for building this managerial philosophy are attitudes and beliefs about people and about the managerial role, not manuals and forms.

Often such a development of management by integration and self-control begins with an individual who develops his own strategy and discovers its value. Soon, his subordinates are following his example, and before long others around him are asking questions and considering their own applications of the idea. If the initial steps are taken by a manager toward the top of the organization, the growth of the idea may be more rapid, but the process can start anywhere. As interest begins to be shown by others, the staff will often face the problem of persuading management that this is not a new gimmick and of fending off demands for the formal machinery which is so often seen as the only requirement for a new personnel program.

Managers who have undertaken to manage by integration and self-control report that the strategy is time-consuming. Roles cannot be clarified, mutual agreement concerning the responsibilities of a subordinate's job cannot be reached in a few minutes, nor can appropriate targets be established without a good deal of discussion. It is far quicker to hand a subordinate a position description and to inform him of his objectives for the coming period. If, however, the strategy is perceived as a way of managing which requires less policing of subordinates and which is accompanied by growth in managerial competence, the expenditure of time will be accepted as natural.

This approach does not tack a new set of duties on top of the existing managerial load. It is, rather, a different way of fulfilling existing responsibilities—of "running the job." I have yet to meet a manager who has made effective use of this managerial strategy who is critical of the time required. Several have said, "If this isn't the primary job of the manager, what is?"

6

A Critique of Performance Appraisal

It will be instructive to contrast the strategy of management by integration and self-control with a more familiar one utilizing performance appraisals. Performance appraisal is often perceived simply as a technique of personnel administration, but where it is used for administrative purposes it becomes part of a managerial strategy, the implicit logic of which is that in order to get people to direct their efforts toward organizational objectives, management must tell them what to do, judge how well they have done, and reward or punish them accordingly. This strategy varies in detail from company to company, but in general it includes the following steps:

1. A formal position description, usually prepared by staff groups, which spells out the responsibilities of the job, determines the limits of authority, and thus provides each individual with a clear picture of what he is supposed to do.

2. Day-by-day direction and control by the superior within the limits of the formal position description. The superior

assigns tasks, supervises their performance and, of course, is expected to give recognition for good performance and criticize poor performance, correct mistakes, and resolve difficulties in the day-to-day operation.

3. A periodic, formal summary of the subordinate's performance by the superior, using some kind of a standardized rating form. Typically, the rating will include judgments concerning the quantity and quality of the subordinate's work; his attitudes toward his work and toward the company (loyalty, cooperativeness, etc.); such personality characteristics as his ability to get along with others, his judgment, and his reactions under stress; and over-all judgments of his "potential" and of his readiness for promotion.

4. A session in which the superior communicates his judgments to the subordinate, discusses the reason for them, and advises the subordinate on ways in which he needs to improve.

5. The subsequent use of the formal appraisal by others in the administration of salaries, promotions, management development programs, etc.

Variations of these procedures are utilized to improve the objectivity of the superior's judgments, to increase comparability of judgment among different superiors, and to improve the fineness of discrimination. For example, some plans utilize multiple judgments obtained independently from several superiors or developed in a group setting; some utilize the "forced choice" method in which a series of quite specific judgments are translated into general scores (the superior does not know the weighting of individual items and presumably does not know how he has evaluated the subordinate until the results are calculated). Many companies conduct programs for training superiors in rating procedures and in counseling techniques.

Appraisal programs are designed not only to provide more systematic control of the behavior of subordinates, but also to control the behavior of superiors. For example, it is believed that an appraisal program will force the superior to face up to problems of poor performance and deal with them, that it will force him to communicate to his subordinates his judgments of their performances, etc.

A considerable amount of experience has accumulated with respect to the way in which this general strategy tends to work out in practice. How well does it achieve its purposes? Let us see.

The Position Description

First, formal position descriptions provide management with an orderly picture of the organization and the comfortable conviction that people know what they are supposed to do. They establish formal chains of command and they delimit authority so that people will not interfere with each other. Position descriptions are a basis for an equitable salary classification scheme, provided it is recognized that at best they yield only a rough picture of reality. However, they are not a particularly realistic device for telling people what to do. Within the managerial hierarchy it is doubtful that any job is performed the same by two successive incumbents, or by the same incumbent over any long period of time. Not only do conditions change, but so do skills and relative abilities, and perceptions of priorities. Companies would utilize less of their human resources than they now do if managers were to adjust to their position descriptions rather than the other way around.

Management at middle and lower levels makes little actual use of position descriptions. Typically, they are glanced over when they are received in order to determine whether they coincide with common-sense preconceptions, and then they are filed away and forgotten. Many research studies show up substantial differences in the perceptions of subordinates and superiors concerning the requirements and priorities of the positions of the former. Position descriptions do not often produce the clarity of understanding they are designed to provide.

Organizations which really attempt to use position descriptions for control purposes (government agencies, for example) stimulate a substantial amount of managerial behavior the primary purpose of which is to defeat the system. The juggling of position descriptions by managers to enable them to do what they want to do— hire a particular person who does not fit a classification, make a salary adjustment, legitimize a promotion—is a common phenomenon in such organizations. The neat systems are often rendered ineffective by these countermeasures.

Organization planning groups sometimes attempt to eliminate these difficulties by a participative approach in which individual incumbents of jobs are encouraged to help the staff by contributing their own knowledge to the writing of the job description. While this process undoubtedly reduces the resistance to the whole idea, it is doubtful whether it results in greater use of the position descriptions themselves for direction and control of behavior.

The dimensions of a managerial position can be precisely defined only for a particular incumbent in a particular set of circumstances at a given point in time. Among the variables which affect the "shape" of the position are the following:

1. The way in which superiors, subordinates, and colleagues are performing their jobs. The position of a sales vice president, for example, will be vastly different if the president of the organization has had his major exprience in sales than it will if the president's experience has been in research or in manufacturing.

2. The individual's qualifications. These include his experience and competence which change over time and thus lead him to perceive the requirements of his position differently and to perform differently.

3. The individual's personal interests. These are related to, but not identical with, his qualifications.
4. The individual's assumptions about his role as a manager. His position will be different depending upon the degree to which he delegates responsibility, for example.
5. The constantly changing requirements of the external situation. Economic conditions, peculiarities of the market, political circumstances, competitive conditions, and a host of other variables require changes in performance which affect the nature of the job.

At two different points in time, perhaps a year apart, a given position might change from being like Figure 1 to being like Figure 2.

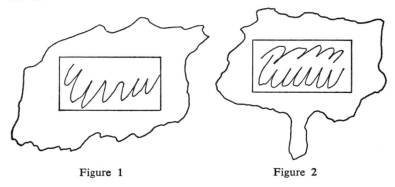

Figure 1   Figure 2

Meanwhile, the formal position description is likely to continue to look like the rectangle in the figures. Even when there are attempts to keep position descriptions up to date and to relate them closely to the incumbents' views of their responsibilities, the variations in the real dimensions of the jobs are rarely captured.

Apart from providing guides for salary administration and some help in hiring and placement, the chief values of position descriptions are (1) to satisfy the needs of organization planners for order and systematization, and (2) to provide reassurance to top management that everyone has a piece of paper which tells him what to do. The danger is that both these groups will make the mistake of assuming that the descriptions represent reality.

Appraisal: The Administrative Purpose

Let us consider now how well the appraisal process itself achieves its purposes. One of these purposes is administrative: the results of appraisal are used for salary administration, promotion, transfer, demotion, and termination. There are difficulties here, too.

In the first place, the problem of variation in the standards of different judges has never been completely solved, nor have we succeeded in eliminating the effects of bias and prejudice in making appraisal judgments. These variations among judges will be greater or smaller depending upon the particular method of appraisal used (whether it involves multiple judgments, for example) and the amount of training given in its use, but they remain substantial nevertheless. The answer given by an appraisal form to the question: "How has A done?" is as much a function of the superior's psychological make-up as of the subordinate's performance.

If we then take these somewhat questionable data and attempt to use them to make fine discriminations between people for purposes of salary administration and promotion, we can create a pretty picture, but one which has little relation to reality. Using fairly simple procedures, and some safeguards against extreme bias and prejudice, it is probably fair to say that we can discriminate between the outstandingly good, the satisfactory, and the unsatisfactory performers. When, however, we attempt to use the results of appraisal to make discriminations much finer than this, we are quite probably deluding ourselves. The fact is that many salary administration and promotion plans use appraisal results to make discriminations considerably smaller than the margin of error of the original judgments.

The problem of judging performance for administrative purposes is further complicated by the fact that any individual's performance is, to a considerable extent, a function of how he is managed. For example, the individual who operates best when he is given quite a bit of freedom may find himself under a superior who provides close and detailed supervision. Under these conditions, even the most objective measures of his performance will provide a better basis for judging his boss than him!

Finally, it is relatively easy to find evidence that the judgments which managers make of their subordinates' performances differ depending upon whether they are used for administrative purposes.

One company used formal appraisals for several years simply as a basis for consultation between the superior and his subordinates. The appraisal forms were kept in a central file, but with the understanding that they would not be used for any administrative purpose.

As a result of certain changes in top management, a concern developed that there was too much "deadwood" in the managerial organization of this company. The staff were instructed to go through the appraisal forms in the central file in order to locate individuals who had, over a period of time, showed no particular improvement in performance, and the managers of these individuals were instructed to do something to change this behavior or terminate the relationship. It was further announced that the periodic appraisals would henceforth be used for administrative purposes.

The next set of appraisals showed a drastic revision upward. Most of the "deadwood" had disappeared from the distribution, although not from the organization. Thus, top management's attempt to control through the appraisals brought about a change, but not quite the one that had been intended.

It would seem to be a fair generalization that performance appraisals are something less than a perfect tool for administering salaries, promotions, transfers, and terminations. What about their value in achieving their informative purpose? Are they an adequate means for letting the subordinate know where he stands?

Appraisal: The Informative Purpose

It is characteristic of human beings that they find it difficult to hear and accept criticism. Judgments which are positive can perhaps be communicated effectively, but it is rather difficult to communicate critical judgments without generating defensiveness.

This difficulty with the appraisal interview is well illustrated by a common dilemma. If the superior attempts to communicate his criticism in the form of abstractions and generalities, he is likely to be asked to be more specific, to give illustrations. The subordinate feels that the generalizations do not give him a sufficient basis for correcting his behavior. If, on the other hand, the superior attempts to communicate in terms of concrete illustrations, he is likely to find himself on the defensive as the subordinate attempts to show that there were extenuating circumstances surrounding any illustration which he brings up.

In attempting to communicate criticisms to a subordinate the superior usually finds that the effectiveness of the communication is inversely related to the subordinate's need to hear it. The more serious the criticism, the less likely is the subordinate to accept it. If the superior is insistent enough, he may be able to convey his negative judgments to a subordinate, but when this happens he often finds that he has done serious damage to the relationship between them. Since the appraisal interview is an important occasion during which the attempt is made to give the subordinate a rather complete evaluation, it carries substantial overtones for him. It accentuates his dependence and thus readily arouses latent anxieties and hostilities. Critical judgments in this setting mean far more than when they are made with respect to specific incidents in the day-to-day relationship. Criticism of the latter type does not threaten the person himself as do the more general evaluative judgments communicated in connection with a formal appraisal, and thus they are easier to hear and respond to.

It is an open question whether subordinates in general really want to know where they stand. It is true that when asked, the great majority will insist that they do want to know. However, it is possible to interpret this expressed desire in several ways. It may mean, for example, "I don't know whether my boss feels I am doing an adequate job because he says so little about my performance in our day-to-day relationship. I feel I am doing well, and I would certainly like to know whether he feels the same way." This is not necessarily the desire for a cold-blooded, objective evaluation. It may be an expression of anxiety and of a need for reassurance. If, in fact, the individual is doing well, and the evaluation involves only minor criticisms, the appraisal interview may fill the need. If the individual is not doing well, the interview will intensify the anxiety and make it extremely difficult for him to react realistically.

The expressed desire to know where he stands may, for another individual, mean, "I know that I am doing a relatively poor job in some respects, but I hope the boss is not aware of it. I would like to be sure this is the case." Still another meaning might be, "I know I am doing an outstanding job, and I would like more recognition for it from the boss. He doesn't seem to be aware of how good I am."

These and many other attitudes are the natural consequence of the situation in which the responsibility for evaluation rests, not on the individual himself, but on the boss. If our managerial strategy emphasizes this childlike dependence, this schoolboy reliance on teacher's grade, we should not be surprised if the reactions to an objective appraisal are sometimes immature.

There is still another aspect of the appraisal interview as a communications device. Since most appraisals involve the superior's evaluation of attitudes and personality traits, in addition to objective performance, there is an invitation inherent in the situation to invade the personality of the subordinate. Recognizing the delicacy of this situation, many managements encourage the superior to use the interview for "counseling" purposes.

It can be stated categorically that few managers are competent to practice psychotherapy. Moreover, the situation of the appraisal interview, in which the superior is in the role of a judge, is the poorest possible one for counseling. The effective counseling relationship is one in which the counselor is a neutral party who neither criticizes nor praises, and whose concern is solely for the health and well-being of the client. To attempt to counsel in a formal appraisal interview is as much a travesty as to attempt bribery of a victim during a holdup. The manager, in making judgments about a subordinate, is implying that he needs to change his behavior in certain ways, and clearly in the minds of both is the recognition that the superior is in a position to punish him if he does not change. Surely this is not a situation for effective counseling, even if the superior is skilled in psychotherapy. The role of judge and the role of counselor are incompatible.

Appraisal: The Motivational Purpose

Finally, consider the motivational purpose of appraisal. The common-sense assumption is that telling an individual where he is falling down will provide effective motivation to get him to change. Clearly it will not do so unless he accepts the negative judgment and agrees with it. We have already seen that this is not too likely a possibility. Contrast the situation in which a subordinate is evaluating his own performance relative to specific targets which he set a few months ago with the situation in which he is listening to his superior evaluate his performance against the superior's standards and objectives. In the latter case, the stage is set for rationalization, defensiveness, inability to understand, reactions that the superior is being unfair or arbitrary. These are not conditions conducive to effective motivation.

The semiannual or annual appraisal is not a particularly efficient stimulus to learning for another reason: It provides "feedback" about behavior at a time remote from the behavior itself. People do learn and change as a result of feedback. In fact, it is the only way they learn. However, the most effective feedback occurs immediately after the behavior. The subordinate can learn a great deal from a mistake, or a particular failure in performance, provided it is analyzed while all the evidence is immediately at hand. Three or four months later, the likelihood of effective learning from that experience is small. It will be still smaller if the superior's generalized criticism relates to several incidents spread over a period of months.

Finally, it is common experience that managers tend to resist and avoid the task of making formal appraisals, and particularly of conducting appraisal interviews when critical judgments are involved. Somehow, the task is an onerous one. Many managers recognize the difficulties described above, and their resistance is due to a realistic skepticism about the whole procedure. Whatever the reasons, it is unlikely that the superior will perform a disliked task in a mannner which will motivate and encourage the subordinate to become more effective. Once more, it seems that a means of control—in this instance control of the superior—through the procedure of the formal appraisal and interview is inappropriate. It does not represent selective adaptation to human nature.

It should be pointed out that many managers, guided by assumptions like those of Theory Y, have invented adaptations of conventional appraisal procedures which avoid some of the difficulties discussed above.

As one simple and relatively effective example, a chief engineer in a large manufacturing organization which has a typical appraisal program distributes copies of the appraisal form to his subordinates every six months with this comment: "Why don't you fill this out on yourself from your knowledge of how you have performed during these few months. I'll fill one out on you independently. If we agree, we won't need to worry about much of an appraisal interview. If we disagree, we can get together and thrash out our differences."

Of course this "gimmick" in the hands of an exponent of Theory X could be a devastating weapon! As used by this man in the light of his philosophy of management, however, it is a rather effective countermeasure to the impact of the appraisal machinery as it is administered in his company.

The theoretical assumptions of Theory X lead quite naturally to a strategy of telling people what to do, judging their performance, and rewarding or punishing them, and to procedures such as those involved in performance appraisal. It appears to be something of a tribute to the adaptability of human beings that these procedures work at all. The main point, however, is that the managerial strategy underlying them is not particularly appropriate for controlling human behavior in the setting of industry today. Certainly, the strategy of management by integration and self-control is more appropriate for intelligent adults and is more likely to be conducive to growth, learning, and improved performance.

REFERENCES

Drucker, Peter F., "Integration of People and Planning, *Harvard Business Review*, vol. 33, no. 6 (November–December), 1955.

Foundation for Research on Human Behavior, *Performance Appraisal and Review*. Ann Arbor, Mich.: 1958.

Kelly, Philip R., "Reappraisal of Appraisals," *Harvard Business Review*, vol. 36, no. 3 (May–June), 1958.

Mahler, Walter R., and Guyot Frazier, "Appraisal of Executive Performance: The 'Achilles Heel' of Management Development," *Personnel*, vol. 31, no. 5, 1955.

Maier, Norman R. F., *The Appraisal Interview*. New York: John Wiley & Sons, Inc., 1958.

Rowland, Virgil K., "From the Thoughtful Businessman," *Harvard Business Review*, vol. 35, no. 5 (September–October), 1957.

Whisler, Thomas L., "Performance Appraisal and the Organization Man," *The Journal of Business*, vol. 31, no. 1 (January), 1958.

7

Administering Salaries
and Promotions

It will not be surprising if the reader is saying at this point: "Yes, but what about the practical problems connected with administering salaries and promotions? It is all very nice to be informal and to encourage managers to avoid the difficult task of making judgments about their subordinates. How are the necessary decisions going to be made concerning problems, transfers, terminations? How are we to decide who gets a salary increase, or an executive bonus, and how much? Does self-appraisal mean self-determination of income and self-placement?"

These are legitimate questions. In order to see that they have at least partial answers, it will be necessary to examine the conventional approach to wage and salary administration and to promotion and placement.

Wage and Salary Administration

Within the framework of Theory X, the ability to provide or withhold economic rewards is the prime means by which management exercises authority in industry. Money is perceived as the major motivator of human behavior in the organizational setting. Money is a means for satisfying many needs. This fact enables management to use it to obtain acceptance of direction and control. The employment contract is perceived as an agreement to accept direction in return for economic rewards.

As we have seen, the existence of a situation of full employment, the relatively high standard of living, the considerable mobility of the population, and the presence of various forms of social legislation all tend to lessen somewhat the degree of dependence of employees today. Money *is* essential for satisfying many needs, but the individual is less dependent upon a single employer for obtaining it than he once was.

The more important question, however, is *how much* money is necessary to make the employment contract effective? This, of course, is a relative matter in several respects. The necessary amount is first of all relative to the competition of the labor market and to general economic conditions including the cost of living, the tax structure, etc. Second, it is relative to the importance of the job in question within the hierarchy of jobs in the organization. Third, it is relative to the contribution of the individual because the "productivity" of individuals on the same job varies.

Establishing the Wage and Salary Structure. Two major considerations determine the nature of managerial policy and practice with respect to wage and salary administration. The first is the consideration of equity: whether the amount of money provided is perceived to be fair relative to the market, economic conditions, the importance of the job, and the individual's contribution. If it is not, either the individual will not take the job, or, having taken it, he wil¹ not perform in a satisfactory manner (he will restrict his output, be indifferent or antagonistic to organizational objectives, engage in countermeasures which interfere with management's attempts to direct and control his behavior).

The second consideration is that of incentive (in the broad sense, including all types of economic rewards): the use of differential increments of money to yield differential increments of effort. In general it is assumed that more money will result in more effort.

In this field of wage and salary administration there is a strong emphasis on measurement because it is recognized that a systematic determination of economic rewards is more equitable than one based on arbitrary decisions, personal considerations, pressure ("the squeaky wheel"), and individual opinion. Arguments, friction, and countermeasures are reduced to the extent that economic rewards can be determined by impersonal and objective methods. Measurement is, therefore, the key to equity in administering economic rewards.

Management's success in achieving equity through the use of measurement varies, depending upon the nature of the problems involved. In the determination of general levels of wages and salaries relative to economic conditions, we encounter some difficult problems which are reduced, but not solved, by systematic approaches. Market surveys, cost-of-living indices, and policies such as that of providing economic benefits "equal to or better than" the average, certainly increase the degree of acceptance. However, questions of the company's "ability to pay" and of the employee's "fair share of the fruits of enterprise" do not lend themselves to determination by formula. Collective and individual bargaining, within a framework of measurement, become the ultimate determinants.

Within the organization, determination of differential wages and salaries for particular jobs is generally accomplished today by wage and salary classification plans which rest on systematic attempts to measure job importance. Management has been reasonably successful in this area. There are, however, some inequities which seem to be impossible to eliminate with present classification methods. For example, the differential between top worker job rates and the rates for the lowest levels of supervisory jobs is a constant source of trouble. Certain kinds of jobs, such as that of the research scientist or the top-level executive are difficult to evaluate. Market conditions sometimes create insurmountable inequities (the current inflation of the market price for technically trained college graduates puts a severe strain on the salary structure).

By and large, however, it has proved possible to achieve a reasonable equity by means of job evaluation and salary classification plans. It has become clear that attempts to achieve ever more precise measurement in this field are not particularly rewarding. The specialists are so enamored of the intricacies of measurement itself that the plans tend to become unintelligible, and suspicion of their adequacy is generated. Equity hinges on acceptance, and relatively simple classification plans appear to be more readily accepted than some of the more elaborately "scientific" ones.

Rewarding Individual Differences in Productivity. The most difficult problems in wage and salary administration arise when we turn to the measurement of individual contributions within the framework of general wage levels and of wage and salary classification. Variations in performance among individuals on any job are substantial, and management continually seeks ways of relating economic rewards to these variations. The major concern is, of course, the motivational one, but it is inextricably tangled with problems of equity.

The wage incentive field yields some instructive insights if we are willing to perceive them. An incredible amount of effort and ingenuity have been directed toward the problem of measuring worker output in order to relate economic rewards to it. Nevertheless, individual incentive plans have never provided the motivation which might be expected on logical grounds. Problems of equity plague management continually, and the costs involved in trying to alleviate them are so high that many managements have abandoned incentive plans in favor of measured day work. It has been impossible so far to prove conclusively which approach is better, but it is clear that the gains for the organization from individual incentive plans are modest even under the best conditions.

For salaried employees (including managers), merit rating plans take the place of incentive plans as a method of providing differential economic rewards for individual contributions. Measurement here becomes an even more difficult matter. Except in the limited number of instances where direct measures of profit and loss can be utilized, the criterion for the individual's contribution is uncertain.

The most carefully designed systematic attempts at measurement of individual contribution (and these are few and far between!) are usually based on over-all subjective ratings or rankings of performance. These are then correlated with specific characteristics of performance which can be judged, and a rating form is developed, utilizing the items which correlate best with the over-all rankings. The correlations are rarely high enough to account for more than half the variance in performance, even when many items are combined. Moreover, even if the correlations are high, they are correlations with a criterion of performance which is itself subjective (the original ranking).

Few merit rating plans even attempt this degree of scientific precision. Normally, the rating form is a series of variables which are simply assumed without any test whatever to correlate with over-all contribution to the enterprise. They are rated by the individual's superior, weighted (or not) according to arbitrary rules, and combined in some fashion to give a general "measure" of performance. It requires no more than a cursory examination of most such plans to raise serious questions about their validity.

As one illustration, consider a rating form which includes a factor of "loyalty." While it is probably true that active disloyalty is negatively correlated with contribution to the enterprise, does it follow that maximum loyalty represents a positive contribution? Is it not possible that the blindly loyal individual would never even perceive policies or practices or decisions which were poor and sorely needed correction? Does management value most the individual who puts loyalty to the organization above loyalty to his own highest principles?

Similar naïve assumptions are revealed when, for example, "quality" and "control of costs" are rated as independent factors with no recognition that in some sense they are reciprocal.

The problems with merit rating plans are compounded by another consideration, namely, the widespread policy of strict secrecy with respect to individual managerial salaries. Equity—that is, acceptance of the fairness of decisions—cannot rest *alone* on confidence in a system of measurement. It rests also on perceptions of how fairly the system is administered. But here we have a situation in which the plan itself is usually subject to serious questions concerning the adequacy of measurement, and there is an additional requirement of secrecy concerning the results of its administration.

A final complication results from the fact that merit plans are used to make not gross but fine differentiations between individuals. One may receive a 3 per cent increase, another 6 per cent, another 10 per cent. As previously suggested, it is likely that the probable error of measurement of most merit rating plans is several times the magnitude of the differentiations that are made in their administration. Perhaps it is just as well that management attempts to maintain secrecy with respect to the results of its administration of such plans!

In the light of considerations such as these, let us ask some questions: Given an adequate base salary structure, is it in fact likely that small increments of salary provide genuine motivation for increased effort? In view of our earlier consideration of motivation, is it likely that such kinds of limited economic rewards have a fraction of the incentive value that opportunities for increased satisfaction of social, ego, and self-actualization needs would have? Within the present income tax structure, what is the real significance, motivationally speaking, of a 5 or even a 10 per cent salary increase to an individual making $15,000 or $20,000 a year? Is it possible that the assumptions of Theory X have led to reliance on the least appropriate among several alternative methods of influence? To be sure, management can provide or withhold salary increments authoritatively, while it can only create conditions (or fail to) for individuals to achieve satisfaction of their higher-level needs. However, would it not seem that emphasis on the principle of integration in contrast to authoritative control of relatively minor increments of economic reward, might merit exploration?

Conclusions. The conclusions which seem to me reasonable with respect to salary administration are these:

1. The problems of equity with respect to economic rewards can be reasonably solved by systematic market survey, attention to the cost of living, policies such as paying salaries "equal to or better than" average, well-conceived position classification plans, and the processes of collective and individual bargaining. In this fashion the individual can be assured of a general level of economic reward which he will accept as fair.

2. The problems of motivation will be solved in part by the provision of equitable rewards in the form of base salaries and in part by providing opportunities for achieving satisfaction of higher-level needs through efforts directed

toward organizational objectives (the principle of integration).

3. Four categories of increments of economic reward above base salaries are realistic:

   a. Those that can be directly tied to objective criteria of accomplishment such as profit and loss. These will necessarily be limited to a few people in the total population if they are administered on an individual basis. Moreover, they will, potentially, be large enough to have genuine motivational value.

   b. Those that are administered as "time-service" increments, received automatically at intervals so long as performance is not unsatisfactory. Such increments will be small, and will have as their chief value the maintenance of equity (on the assumption that time on a job brings some increase in competence and in contribution).

   c. Merit increases to the small proportion of individuals in a given salary classification whose performance is clearly *outstanding*. These will require only gross differentiations of performance in which the probable error of measurement will be small, and they will also involve large enough salary increments to have genuine motivational value.

   d. Group rewards for departmental, or divisional, or company-wide achievement of objectively measurable economic results. These would be shared within the group in terms of an equal percentage of base salary. (The Scanlon Plan, to be considered in Chapter 8, utilizes this method of motivating performance.)

4. Conventional programs for providing large numbers of people with differential and relatively small merit salary increases, in the light of our present ability to measure managerial contributions to the enterprise, are not very

realistic. The absence of objective criteria of performance and the problems involved in measurement are such that equity cannot be achieved through such methods. Moreover, there is reason to doubt that such rewards have much motivational value relative to other opportunities which can be provided through applications of the principle of integration.[1]

Thus the question about salary administration raised at the beginning of this chapter is answered: *It is unnecessary for the superior to make the judgments we have customarily relied upon to administer economic rewards* (except possibly with respect to a few individuals whose performance is outstanding). For some, these conclusions will appear defeatist. They are, if one stays within the framework of Theory X. From the point of view of Theory Y, they suggest simply that we have been relying on inappropriate methods of control. Conventional merit plans of salary administration do not represent selective adaptation to the conditions we face. The challenge is to find other ways to motivate people. Management by integration and self-control offers one such method.

There is no implication in this conclusion that economic rewards are unimportant. The implication is that an equitable salary struc-

---

[1] The previously mentioned study of Herzberg, Mausner, and Snyderman, supports the conclusion in this paragraph. The writers point out that when salary was a factor in producing dissatisfaction, it was associated with "the unfairness of the wage system within the company, and this almost always referred to increases in salaries rather than the absolute levels. It was the system of salary administration that was being described, a system in which wage increases were obtained grudgingly, or given too late, or in which the differentials between newly hired employees and those with years of experience on the job were too small." On the other hand, salary increases were a source of satisfaction primarily as they accompanied job achievements. They conclude: "It would seem that as an affector of job attitudes salary has more potency as a job dissatisfier than as a job satisfier." Herzberg, Mausner, and Snyderman, *The Motivation to Work*, pp. 82–83.

ture furnishes the major economic rewards, but that our attempts to get greater "productivity" *through the use of small increments of economic reward within such a structure* have not been particularly effective.

The Administration of Promotions and Placement

Unfortunately, it does not seem possible to solve the problems involved in promotion by eliminating the necessity for subjective judgments by superiors of their subordinates. Moreover, in addition to considerations of equity and motivation, there are considerations of qualifications involved. What experience and training, what abilities and skills are required to perform a given job, and how can we determine which individual among several candidates possesses these to the greatest degree?

It is tempting to assume that these problems would be solved if we could develop adequate methods for measuring (1) jobs and (2) individual qualifications (in contrast to individual contributions to the enterprise). Much time and effort has been and is being devoted to the pursuit of this objective. Many staff specialists have the dream of a system which would involve a set of punched cards carrying the detailed requirements of every job and another set carrying the qualifications of every member of the organization. Filling openings would then require only a mechanical process of matching. However, as in the case of measuring merit, there are formidable obstacles.

We noted in the previous chapter that jobs—and particularly managerial jobs—do not consist of fixed receptacles whose detailed dimensions can be measured. They are embedded in complex organizational and external relationships which change substantially over time. In addition, it is simply not true that one and only one pattern of qualifications of the incumbent will yield the best performance of a given job. Variations in personal qualifications will result in the job being performed *differently,* but several such patterns could lead to equivalent results as far as the achievement of organizational objectives is concerned.

Conventional organization theorists usually lay great stress on defining the job and then fitting an individual to it. They are concerned to prevent the "square peg in the round hole." Such an idea may have the merit of logical simplicity, but the fact that this rule is so rarely followed in practice should warn us that the problem is considerably more complex than this. Moreover, the principle of integration is sharply contradictory to the conception that the individual must be adapted and molded to the requirements of the organization.

Further, while progress is being made, we are still a long way even from knowing what the qualifications for managerial success in most jobs may be, let alone from being able to measure them. Finally, since personality characteristics and factors of emotional adjustment are thought to be as important as factors of experience, training, skill, and intellectual capacity, we must face the ethical problem which was briefly mentioned in Chapter 1. There is a real question concerning the ethics of using private and personal data (in contrast to "public" data on performance, educational achievement, etc.) in administering promotions and placement.

Certainly the dream of a mechanical matching of job characteristics and personal qualifications has no more than very limited possibilities. For the foreseeable future, managerial judgments of a subjective kind are going to play a large part in administering promotions and placements.

A Role for Measurement. Research groups in several companies have developed methods of measurement for selection and for promotion with respect to a limited number of positions which have given management substantial help. A rather elaborate procedure is necessary for each position, and hence the method is useful only when there is continuing need for numbers of candidates. It does not lend itself to the situation where replacements on a given job are infrequent, or where the number of incumbents is small.

The research involves the determination by statistical means of a large number of "items" (aspects of experience, attitude, ability, personality) which discriminate between present incumbents of the position who are ranked by management on the basis of overall value to the company. These items are combined in a test (with weights determined by their discriminative value) which is then used to help screen applicants.

There is evidence that this procedure can improve selection and promotion practices materially *provided:*

1. Management becomes actively involved in the research leading to the development of the tests (and thus acquires a real understanding both of the values and the limitations of the instruments).

2. The tests are used as an aid to selection and not as the sole basis for judgment. (It is easy to obtain lip service to this principle, but hard to maintain it in practice because the tendency is to rely on the test scores. This is one reason why management participation in the research is important.)

3. The conception of "good" and "poor" performance remains unchanged. (Since the whole approach hinges on management's original ranking of incumbents, the tests discriminate *only in terms of that criterion.* If the requirements of the job change, or if management acquires a different idea of what constitutes "good" performance, the tests become useless and the research must be repeated.)

Even this rather elaborate research method does not eliminate managerial judgment in the administration of promotion and placement. Nevertheless, the use of standardized tests and procedures (without such custom-tailored methods) as the primary basis for

selection in filling complex managerial jobs is not uncommon today. Many commercial firms offer services of this kind. The evidence for the validity of such methods is dubious, to say the least.
(This is one more reason for concern with the ethics of managerial practices in this field. The manager is likely to feel some
responsibility in making subjective judgments which affect the
career of a fellow human being. Most of us are a little hesitant
about "playing God." When, however, one can let the decision
rest on a "scientific" determination, it is all too easy to slough
off the responsibility.)

Whether or not tests are utilized, there are safeguards in the
form of procedures which can help to improve the validity of
managerial judgments and which will help to protect the individual against the consequences of prejudice, poor judgment, and the
like. Carefully designed methods for utilizing group judgments represent the best of these.

The Role of the Individual. Perhaps the biggest change required
in current practices with respect to promotion and placement—
if we desire to utilize the principle of integration—has to do with
the relation of the "candidate" to the process. Today he tends to
be a pawn on the organizational chessboard. Plans are frequently
made with respect to his career which may have profound effects
upon his most important goals and needs. Yet he is likely to have
no voice in these plans and to remain in complete ignorance of
them until after the decision has been reached. Moreover, the organization's needs are given priority almost without consideration
of his needs. If his goals and needs are considered at all, it is
likely to be in the paternalistic sense of deciding "what is good
for him."

An assistant chief engineer, aged thirty-eight, in a large
organization, has for several years desired some line experience. He has expressed a strong interest in a job where he
could have a reasonable autonomy and be judged by "the

p. and 1. statement." He has shown considerable administrative ability in the various engineering jobs he has held. He is regarded by those above him as outstanding, and a likely prospect some day for vice president of engineering.

In a discussion with a manager two levels above him who has had both interest and influence on this man's career, I asked if he had ever been considered for a line job. The answer was emphatic: "Oh, no! His forte is engineering."

The principle of integration requires active and responsible participation of the individual in decisions affecting his career. However radical this may be, however impractical it may seem in the light of traditional practice, it is a requirement if we would create conditions such that the individual can achieve his own goals best by directing his efforts toward organizational objectives. No amount of scientific evidence concerning his qualifications, no safeguards to ensure sound and unprejudiced judgments, no rationalizations about the disappointment of unsuccessful candidates can justify excluding the individual from a process which is so important to him.

A beginning can be made in target-setting sessions. Here it is feasible to discuss the individual's career interests, to consider needed experiences and training, kinds of opportunities which would be relevant, questions of timing. Here, too, personal considerations which might affect his desire to move from his present job or to stay on it can be discussed.

One company has had a practice for several years of asking each member of management, periodically: "Is your hat in the ring?" If his answer is yes, he is considered for relevant openings which may occur. If it is no, he is excluded from such considerations *without prejudice*. Of course, the question will be asked again in a year or two, and he may feel differently then. The decision, however, is his.

Data about the individual's interests, his relevant experience, and even his capacities as measured by tests can, with his full knowledge and agreement, be included in the central personnel file for possible reference as openings occur. The results of personality tests and clinical evaluations, *provided they are kept confidential between the psychologist and the individual,* can be a basis on which he plans his career and decides whether to be a candidate for particular openings.

A few companies have developed procedures which make it possible for individuals to submit their names as candidates for particular openings. This enables the individual to take a responsible role with respect to his own career development. There are problems involved, of course, but it is possible to find a middle ground between administrative practices which treat the individual as a pawn and those sometimes found at the worker level which involve direct "bidding" for jobs.

In the context of management by integration and self-control, both the superior and the subordinate can furnish data for the administration of promotions. If the superior's judgments differ sharply from those developed by the subordinate's self-appraisals, there will be the need for discussion and resolution of the differences. There is reason to expect, however, that such differences can usually be reconciled during the course of a series of target-setting and self-appraisal discussions.

While I was President of Antioch College, we worked out a review procedure under which any promotional decision made by me which was felt by the faculty member to be unfair could be taken to a faculty board for a hearing and a final decision. Since I was not a member of the review board, this meant that my decision could be overruled.

In the course of about four years during which this system was in operation, only two cases went to the review board. I was upheld on one of these, overruled on the other. My feeling was that this mechanism provided a valuable check against the fallibility of administrative judgments; odd as it may seem, the decision which went against me served to strengthen rather than weaken my position with my faculty. Certainly the very presence of this procedure, even though it was rarely used, lessened the feelings of dependence in the relationships and made it easier for me to deal with difficult situations.

Conclusions. Some general conclusions with respect to the administration of promotions and placement within the context of Theory Y are:

1. The matching of individuals to jobs—at least at managerial levels—cannot be a mechanical process because:
   a. Job requirements are dynamic rather than static; they change as a function of many variables in the situation.
   b. Individuals with different patterns of qualifications, although they may perform a given job differently, can achieve organizational objectives equally well.
   c. We do not have adequate knowledge of the characteristics associated with managerial success, nor very precise methods for measuring those that are considered important.
2. Hence, a considerable element of subjective judgment remains—regardless of the use that is made of measurement —in decisions concerning the placement of individuals. Careful, systematic research can provide tools that will aid judgment, but such tools cannot replace judgment. Exclusive reliance on the results of tests is completely unwarranted at the present stage of development of such tools.

3. The principle of integration demands an active rather than a passive role for the individual in the administration of promotions and placement. At the very least, data which he can provide concerning his interests, goals, and qualifications can be utilized to permit him to become an active candidate for promotional opportunities under most circumstances. His goals and needs—as perceived by him and not simply by others—can influence decisions affecting his career.

4. Judgments of the superior about his subordinates, developed within a strategy of management by integration and self-control, are likely to be based upon data and experience which will improve their quality.

In the administration of promotions, therefore, we face a situation in which it is unrealistic to relinquish the use of authority. The decisions need not be completely unilateral, but they must be made. In the absence of truly objective criteria of performance, there is a substantial degree of dependence of the individual upon those above him. Given this dependence, the exercise of authority is an appropriate means of control *provided we are aware of the negative consequences if equity is not preserved.* Under some conditions it may be feasible to establish review procedures which will serve as a check against arbitrary decisions and thus increase the likelihood of achieving equity.

The answer to the questions raised at the beginning of this chapter is that unilateral direction and control with respect to the administration of salaries and promotions can be reduced but not eliminated (1) by the use of measurement *where it is appropriate,* (2) by eliminating differentiations between individuals when the error of measurement is large and the motivational value of the differentiations is small, and (3) by giving individuals greater opportunities to play an active part in decisions affecting their careers.

Addendum

I can offer no easy solution to the ethical problems involved in the use of test data and clinical personality diagnoses for administrative purposes. The issues are exceedingly complex, but a few comments may be in order.

First, it seems to me that a distinction can be made between test data concerning intellectual aptitudes and capacities on the one hand, and those concerning personality characteristics on the other. Certainly measurement of the latter is still quite primitive, but the critical point is whether management has any moral right to invade the personality. Management's legitimate concern is with performance. Obviously performance is affected by personality characteristics and adjustment, but the question is whether management has a right to go behind the performance to the diagnosis of its causes *when those causes are personal and private.*

The difficulty, of course, is that the restriction imposed by this protection of the individual severely limits the data which can be used for prediction of success or failure on the job. The real reason for management interest in information about the personality is the possibility of improving such predictions. We are interested in an individual's inferiority feelings, or anxieties, or neurotic tendencies because of what they lead us to expect about his performance in given situations. It can even be argued that such knowledge would enable us to protect him from failure and unhappiness, and to protect others from harmful consequences of his personal adjustment.

Yet the use of such knowledge in these ways seems to me to be manipulative in the worst sense of the word. It is permitting the organization to step into the private domain of the person and make decisions for him which only he has the right to make. (Note that, except under the most extreme conditions, a surgeon does not make the final decision to operate, even to save a patient's life. This is felt to be the inviolate right of the person.)

For the clinical psychologist to share his diagnosis with the individual *on a confidential basis,* advising him concerning the possible consequences for him and others if he attempts certain types of responsibilities, raises no problems. If it were left to the individual in consultation with the psychologist to decide what use to make of personality measurements and diagnoses, we would have a situation comparable to that which obtains between managers and medical departments in many large companies today. We have come to accept the idea that it is the individual's own responsibility, not that of his superiors, to decide how health considerations should affect his career decisions, except in cases like those of the airplane pilot and the locomotive engineer where the public safety is directly involved. The parallel with "mental health" seems to me a fairly good one.

Tests of capacity—intelligence tests, for example—seem somehow to be different in nature, and the implications with respect to their use don't present the same difficulties. A measure of intelligence is less personal and private than a diagnosis of emotional adjustment. It is more like a measurement of height or of job knowledge. The test is composed not of questions about personal habits and private attitudes, but of impersonal problems to be solved. It is a measurement based on *performance.*

Many personality characteristics and aspects of adjustment are subject to modification through individual effort, certain types of education, and psychotherapy. It seems unjust to predict behavior on the basis of measures and diagnoses of such characteristics, and therefore to deny the individual the opportunity to change. If we limit ourselves to the statement that a given form of behavior or aspect of his performance is unsatisfactory, we leave open to him the possibility that he can do something about it.

In the end, I can only confess to a degree of disquiet over the possibilities for manipulation and exploitation of my fellow human beings inherent in the administrative use of personality tests and clinical diagnoses of adjustment for purposes of placement. I view with even greater concern the probability that the predictive value of such instruments will be increased substantially during the next decade or two. The issues involved will then be intensified. This whole field of selection, promotion, and placement presents a substantial challenge to the ethical values of professional management. We cannot afford to dismiss the issues by defending unilaterally the needs of the organization, or to look the other way in the hope that they will go away. If we do either, we run the risk that a growing public concern will lead one day to legislative restrictions further curtailing management's freedom of action. More importantly, we put materialistic economic considerations ahead of ethical ones and thus place ourselves as managers in a position few of us would care to defend.

REFERENCES

American Management Association, *Handbook of Wage and Salary Administration.* New York: 1950.

Belcher, David W., *Wage and Salary Administration.* Englewood Cliffs, N.J.: Prentice-Hall, Inc., 1955.

Employee Relations Department, Esso Standard Oil Company, *Made to Measure.* New York: 1953.

Foundation for Research on Human Behavior, *Assessing Managerial Potential.* Ann Arbor, Mich.: 1958.

Jacques, Elliot, *Measurement of Responsibility.* London: Tavistock Publications, Ltd., 1956.

National Industrial Conference Board, Inc., *Employee Salary Plans in Operation,* Studies in Personnel Policy, no. 100, 1949.

Whyte, William H., Jr., *The Organization Man.* New York: Simon & Schuster, Inc., 1956.

8

The Scanlon Plan

Management by integration and self-control can take many forms. One of the most unusual of these is the Scanlon Plan. Out of his deep interest in union-management cooperation, the late Joseph Scanlon evolved a collaborative strategy which has achieved solid results, in both economic and human terms, in a number of industrial companies. Scanlon died in 1956. His work is being ably carried on at MIT today by his close friend and successor, Frederick Lesieur.

The Scanlon Plan is not a formula, a program, or a set of procedures. It is a way of industrial life—a philosophy of management—which rests on theoretical assumptions entirely consistent with Theory Y. The Scanlon Plan differs from target setting in that it is applied to the whole organization rather than to superior-subordinate pairs or to small groups. However, the underlying strategic considerations are very similar.

The plan embodies two central features which in their operation bring about profound changes in organizational relationships, attitudes, and practices. Scanlon's discovery that these two features would encourage the development of a different set of managerial assumptions about organized human effort represents a social invention of considerable significance. Neither of these features alone would be likely to bring about a major change; linked together, however, they represent a powerful system of organizational "control."

Cost-reduction Sharing

The first feature is a means of sharing the economic gains from improvements in organizational performance. It is not profit sharing in the conventional sense at all, but a unique kind of cost-reduction sharing. It is not a substitute for a normal, competitive wage and salary structure, but is built on top of it.

This method for sharing cost-reduction savings utilizes a ratio between the total manpower costs of the organization and a measure of output such as total sales or value added by manufacture. The latter index in the ratio can only be derived after considerable study and analysis of the particular company, and it is relatively unique to the situation. Allowances are made, of course, for product mix, inventory, work in process, etc. In most companies a ratio can be developed which turns out to have been relatively stable for considerable periods of time. Sharp fluctuations can usually be traced to major technological or economic changes.

This ratio is not seen as an exact, infallible, permanent measure. Careful study of the company's financial records, a good deal of common sense, and a lot of mutual discussion enter into its determination. It is subject to change from time to time, as circumstances warrant, and the history of Scanlon companies indicates that these changes are made without difficulty when the need arises.

Improvement of the ratio represents an over-all economic gain for the organization. Some portion of the resultant savings (sometimes 50 per cent, often 75 per cent, occasionally 100 per cent) are paid to participants in the Plan on a monthly basis as a percentage of their base wages or salaries. Normally, all members of the organization except possibly the very top management group participate in this economic reward for improvement. Such a reward, properly developed, gains genuine acceptance (it is perceived to be equitable) and, in addition, provides genuine motivation. It is a means for promoting collaboration within an interdependent system. Competition is minimized within the organization and maximized with respect to other firms in the industry.

An important characteristic of this method of measurement is that it is directly related to the success of the members in improving the over-all economic success of the organization. The ordinary profit-sharing plan lacks this direct relationship. Profits may reflect circumstances and factors almost completely irrelevant to the efforts of the members of the organization. I knew of an instance a few years ago, for example, where nearly three-quarters of the profits of the enterprise over a period of several years resulted from the manipulations of the treasurer in the raw material market. The profit-sharing bonus paid to the employees of this company had little connection with their contribution to the success of the enterprise.

Employees under a Scanlon Plan, on the other hand, are able to trace directly the results of various changes and innovations, stimulated by their efforts, upon the bonus, and thus to see the connection between their behavior and organizational achievement. The result is a very real and quite sophisticated understanding of the economics of the firm, gained through direct experience. Economic education of the work force is never a problem in a Scanlon factory.

There are many examples in Scanlon companies of profitable orders for products obtained after the employees had persuaded management to bid for the business at prices which appeared initially to be ridiculously low. Given a full understanding of the competitive situation and a knowledge of existing costs, the members of the organization were willing to exercise their ingenuity to help management put itself in a strong competitive position. Commitment to the economic objectives of the enterprise is clearly evident at every level and in every function of these companies.

A third feature of the economic reward is that it is reasonably well related temporally to the behavior which produced it. An annual profit-sharing bonus is a reward which has little relationship to daily behavior. A monthly payment carries with it a psychologically meaningful cause-and-effect connection because the behavior and the reward are reasonably close together in time.

Effective Participation

If the Scanlon Plan consisted of nothing but this measure of organizational effectiveness and the bonus, there would be some reason for singling it out for special attention because of the features mentioned above, but fundamentally it would simply be another example of the many varieties of incentive and profit-sharing plans found in industry today. The distinguishing feature of the Scanlon Plan is the coupling of this incentive with a second feature: a formal method providing an opportunity for every member of the organization to contribute his brains and ingenuity as well as his physical effort to the improvement of organizational effectiveness. This is the integrative principle in operation. It is the means by which rich opportunities are provided every member of the organization to satisfy his higher-level needs through efforts directed toward the objectives of the enterprise.

Even the repetitive worker at the bottom of the hierarchy is potentially more than a pair of hands. He is a human resource. His know-how and ingenuity, properly utilized, may make a far greater difference to the success of the enterprise than any improvement in his physical effort, although of course his effort is not unimportant. Moreover, he achieves recognition and other important social and ego satisfactions from this utilization of his capacities.

We hear a great deal of talk about improved productivity and its significance in our total economic picture. Many of those who talk the loudest conceive of productivity solely in terms of the physical output of production and clerical workers. If such people would only do more of what they are told to do, productivity would rise and the economy would be better off. This message is to be heard on every hand today. It is a true virtue of the Scanlon Plan that it scraps completely this narrow and insulting conception of the worth of the human being in the industrial enterprise. Productivity is seen in terms of the over-all effectiveness of the organization, and everything that contributes to it is valued. The distinctive potential contribution of the human being in contrast to the machine, *at every level of the organization,* stems from his capacity to think, to plan, to exercise judgment, to be creative, to direct and control his own behavior. In contrast to the philosophy of traditional incentive plans and the conventional practices of industrial engineering, the Scanlon Plan encourages *and rewards* the distinctively human contribution.

The mechanics of the second feature of the Scanlon Plan consists in a series of committees whose purpose is to receive, discuss, and evaluate every means that anyone can think of for improving the ratio, and to put into effect those that are considered to be workable. Representatives from every group and function in the organization serve on these committees. Departmental committees of workers and lower-level supervision are empowered to put into effect ideas appropriate to their level. Those suggestions which have broader implications are referred to a higher level "screening committee" consisting of representatives of the work force and of higher management.

While this machinery provides channels for evaluation and action, the formalities of its operation are minimal. The committees may meet at regular intervals, but at the departmental level, at least, a committee "meeting" may consist of a five-minute discussion between three or four people on the factory floor, which is followed by adoption of an idea. Minutes of formal meetings are kept to ensure that ideas are not lost and that the screening committee is aware of all actions that are taken anywhere in the organization.

In this fashion the concept of participation is given a meaning which everyone can understand. The fact of interdependence is accepted; reliance is placed on the know-how, the ingenuity, the innovativeness of all the human resources of the organization. The mechanics of the participation are relatively unimportant; the underlying assumptions about human beings which are reflected are crucial.

Participation in Scanlon companies is greatly different from that obtained with conventional suggestion plans. There are no forms to fill out, no impersonal "suggestion boxes," no remote committees to evaluate the merits of the idea in secret. The individual in his own work setting, or at a meeting of the screening committee, discusses his idea, participates in the evaluation of it, obtains recognition if it is a good idea or encouragement to work further on it if it is promising but still impractical. Moreover, he is in a situation which encourages him to seek and obtain help anywhere in the organization in developing the idea rather than one which encourages secrecy in order to prevent someone from stealing his idea and cheating him out of an award. The focus is not on competing for awards but on improving the effectiveness of the enterprise. The economic gains are shared, but the social and ego satisfactions are his alone.

The evidence for the significance of these differences is readily observable in any Scanlon company. There is no need for periodic propaganda campaigns to keep suggestions coming in. Companies which have had suggestion programs for years before the advent of the Scanlon Plan find themselves flooded with economically significant ideas which never appeared before. The proportion of suggestions which get a $5 award, not because they contribute any-thing to the success of the enterprise but because nobody knows what else to do about them, shrinks to zero. Carefully contrived and intelligently developed collaborative studies of organizational problems are common.

In one company the possible savings to be obtained through the use of fork-lift trucks came up for discussion at a department meeting. Out of this discussion there emerged three months later a complete study by a self-appointed group of employees of the savings which could be effected, and a recommendation for purchase based on a penetrating examination of initial and maintenance costs of the various types of lift trucks available. The president of the company commented that he would have had to pay a couple of thou-sand dollars to an outside consultant for an analysis which would have been as thorough and as competent.

Effects on Relations

There are literally hundreds of examples in Scanlon Plan com-panies of improvements in the relationship between functional groups which occur once the Plan gets under way. A single illus-tration will serve to indicate the kind of thing that happens.

In one company there was a substantial amount of fric-tion and antagonism between the work force and the en-gineering department. When workers would discover what they believed to be an error in design, and would call the engineers to bring it to their attention, the stock answer was: "Follow the blueprint."

Since engineers, like all other human beings, are fallible, mistakes did occur. The workers took malicious pleasure in following the blueprint exactly, even though they knew they were making a costly mistake for the company. A common expression among the work force when a piece of equipment went out the door en route to the customer was: "There she goes; she'll be back." The complete lack of confidence either way between workers and engineers led to a considerable amount of behavior inimical to the organization as a whole.

Since the advent of the Scanlon Plan, this relationship has changed. Both groups have a stake in a common objective; they recognize that collaboration toward that objective is to their mutual interest. As a result, a question raised by a worker concerning the correctness of a detail in a blueprint will bring an engineer to the work floor immediately. The engineers have gained considerable respect for the know-how of the work force, and the latter have come to regard the engineers as a genuine source of help.

The changed relationship was evidenced a couple of years after the plan went into effect. The company's business was off, general economic conditions were poor, and there had been some layoffs. A substantial new order was received in the late spring, but the design work on it would take several months. If the normal company practice of shutting down the plant for summer vacation were to be followed, the result would be additional lost time for the work force until the completion of the design work on the new order. Accordingly, the suggestion was made to the screening committee that the engineers change their vacation plans (which naturally included travel reservations, arrangements for renting cottages, etc.) to work on the design through the normal vacation period. The screening committee reaction was that it was a fine idea but that the engineers would never agree to the disruption in their plans. The answer from the group of workers who had submitted the idea was simple and direct: "Oh, we have already talked with the engineers, and they have agreed to shift their plans if you will approve the idea."

The atmosphere in a Scanlon Plan company is not always a peaceful one. There are arguments, disagreements, hot discussions. The distinctive feature of these, however, is that they are almost always centered around the problems of improved performance. Individuals at every level have a stake in the success of the enterprise, and it is a stake which goes well beyond the straight economic rewards that are involved. There is genuine integration, genuine commitment to organizational objectives, because it represents the best way for members to achieve their individual goals, whether these are related to basic biological needs, social needs, egoistic or self-actualization needs. The linking of the two central features of the Scanlon Plan provides a wealth of opportunity for achieving satisfaction of all kinds of human needs. But because human beings differ in their goals and in their perceptions of how best these may be achieved, one finds a normal, healthy disagreement about ways and means. The participative feature of the Plan helps managers to discover the true value of the organization's human resources and in time generates a degree of confidence "downward" which is amazingly different from what one finds in the ordinary company.

These changes in managerial attitude do not always come easily. There is often some tough learning involved, particularly for lower levels of line management. It is not easy for the foreman or the superintendent to adjust to what may seem to him to be a severe loss of power. He is faced squarely with his actual dependence downward and laterally.

As pointed out above, the Plan in operation tends to resolve many of the typical problems of staff-line relationships. While there is frequently a fair amount of initial wear and tear, mutual confidence and collaboration between staff and line eventually develop. Staff groups become resources to the organization rather than policemen. The Plan makes no distinction between "productive" groups and "burden" groups.

The Scanlon Plan cannot be operated on the basis of formulas, gimmicks, or packaged programs. It is truly a way of life, with infinite variations appropriate to the circumstances of the individual company. Scanlon companies reveal the presence of underlying assumptions about human behavior similar to those of Theory Y. The principle of integration receives daily confirmation in practice.

Some Questions

There are several unanswered questions concerning the wider applicability of this philosophy of management which deserve consideration. In the first place, the Plan has so far been applied almost entirely in relatively small companies of a few hundred employees. The largest example is a company of 8,000 employees. Consideration of the way in which the Plan operates indicates that there would be obvious difficulties in applying it to a big organization. The possibility does exist however, of utilizing the Scanlon approach in the context of divisional "profit centers" which are popular among decentralized big companies today.

A more critical question concerns the applicability of the Scanlon philosophy in situations which are highly automated, and where the technology is of a kind that leaves little room for improvement and change originating anywhere but in engineering or research. Some of us who have watched the development of the Scanlon Plan are optimistic about its applicability even under such conditions. The influence of human behavior upon organization success—in maintenance, in construction, in the clerical force, in management generally—even though the operation is highly automated, is more substantial than most people recognize. Sooner or later, an opportunity will come to test this optimism in a real situation. To date, the managements of such companies or divisions have been too skeptical to give the idea a try.

Another question concerns the relation of the Scanlon Plan to general economic conditions. Some of the earlier developments of Scanlon's ideas took place in the depths of the Depression in companies which were either in or on the verge of bankruptcy. Critics of the philosophy were quick to point out that the highly collaborative efforts they observed were a function of the strong motivation of employees to protect their jobs. The conclusion they drew was that the Scanlon Plan might operate under severely depressed economic conditions, but that it would certainly not be successful in boom times. Since the war the Plan has flourished in companies experiencing boom conditions. The critics have argued that, of course, the Plan should be expected to operate successfully when the financial rewards are large, but that it would not operate successfully in a depression!

The point is, of course, that the motivation is different under different economic conditions. This experience of Scanlon companies provides interesting evidence in support of the motivational ideas presented in Chapter 3. There are psychological gains to be realized, regardless of the economic situation of the company. There is an important contrast here again between the Scanlon Plan and the typical profit-sharing plan. Many profit-sharing plans have gone by the board when the economic conditions were such that the profit-sharing bonus was materially reduced or eliminated. In contrast, a number of Scanlon companies have gone through both boom and depression times without losing their underlying commitment. Since the Scanlon Plan is a way of life rather than a particular form of financial incentive plan, one would expect exactly this result.

The point is often raised that successful, efficiently operated companies would be ill-advised to adopt a Scanlon Plan because the possibilities for improving a properly developed ratio would be infinitesimal. It has come as a distinct shock to the top managements of such companies who have adopted the plan that substantial—not minor—improvements have occurred. In one instance the President simply refused to believe that a 20 per cent improvement had occurred until he reexamined in detail all the data on which the ratio had been based. He had been absolutely sure that his company was so efficiently managed that a two or three per cent improvement would be maximal.

Another question concerns the problem of "selling" this philosophy to an organization. Many people believe that the success of the Plan is directly attributable to the remarkable personality of Joseph Scanlon, and that the philosophy could not have been sold and would not have been workable if it had not been for his direct influence. There are today a number of Scanlon companies the members of which never met Joe Scanlon. The plans were installed during Joe's last illness or since his death. Fred Lesieur is indeed a remarkable personality also, but he is a different personality than Joe, and he operates in his own fashion.

It does require a forceful personality somewhere in the situation to help bring about the initial willingness to undertake the risks involved in establishing this new managerial philosophy. Obviously, such a broad shift in managerial philosophy will not occur without skillful leadership. The usual experience has been that such a personality was present inside the organization and that he provided the leadership, while Scanlon or Lesieur has filled the roles of catalyst, teacher, consultant, and sometimes severe critic.

The Scanlon philosophy has been successful in both unionized and nonunionized plants. The presence of an effective union appears to be a positive factor in the success of the Plan. It provides a formal means for communication and discussion during the early stages, particularly in the development of the ratio. It provides a somewhat more organized pressure to keep management "on its toes" as the Plan gets under way. It ensures that there will be no tendency to try to substitute bonus earnings for a competitive wage structure. While there has been an occasional private expression of thought that perhaps successful operation of such a plan would obviate the necessity for collective bargaining, experience has not borne out this prediction. On the contrary, the managements of unionized Scanlon companies tend to be rather more positive about the values of a sound collective bargaining relationship than are many managements in other unionized firms.

One rather significant thing is the complete absence of concern on the part of Scanlon managements over the problem of managerial prerogatives. The protection of their authority is not a central preoccupation. Their confidence in their own employees is such that they feel no defensiveness about their "right to run the business." Given the kind of integration which is characteristic of these companies, the question of control, in the traditional sense, simply ceases to be a meaningful issue.

During discussions which take place in Scanlon Plan Conferences at MIT, managers from companies contemplating adoption of the Plan regularly raise questions about the possible disasters that could occur *if* economic or technological changes dictated a change in the ratio and the employees would not agree to it, or *if* employees took advantage of their access to information about the economic situation of the company, or *if* a variety of other possibilities of employee infringement on managerial prerogatives were to arise.

The fascinating aspect of these discussions is the sheer inability of Scanlon company managements to understand what is worrying the questioners. *Of course* they run their businesses, *of course* they make the essential managerial decisions. Where did the idea originate that the Scanlon Plan weakens management? At the same time they reveal by their examples as well as their attitudes that authority in the conventional sense is not the method of control upon which they rely. Persuasion, logical argument, professional help, the joint recognition of the objective requirements of the situation—these are the influences which determine their behavior and that of the members of their organizations.

In conclusion, it is interesting to note that the issue of individual differentials in economic rewards tied to individual contributions to the success of the company is simply not an issue in these organizations. Many of them have abandoned individual incentive plans in the process of adopting the Scanlon philosophy. In some cases fears were expressed that the high producers would lower their performance under the new arrangements. Not only has this not occurred, but the general level of productivity, measured in the industrial engineer's terms, has almost always increased. The proverbial task of selling refrigerators to Eskimos would be easy compared to the task of selling a traditional incentive plan or a merit rating plan in most Scanlon companies. Both equity and motivation are achieved by more appropriate means.

REFERENCES

Krulee, Gilbert K., "The Scanlon Plan: Cooperation through Participation," *The Journal of Business,* vol. 28, no. 2, 1955.

Lesieur, Frederick G. (ed.), *The Scanlon Plan.* Cambridge, Mass., and New York: Technology Press and John Wiley & Sons, Inc., 1958.

9

Participation in Perspective

Participation is one of the most misunderstood ideas that have emerged from the field of human relations. It is praised by some, condemned by others, and used with considerable success by still others. The differences in point of view between its proponents and its critics are about as great as those between the leaders of Iron Curtain countries and those of the Free World when they use the term "democracy."

Some proponents of participation give the impression that it is a magic formula which will eliminate conflict and disagreement and come pretty close to solving all of management's problems. These enthusiasts appear to believe that people yearn to participate, much as children of a generation or two ago yearned for Castoria. They give the impression that it is a formula which can be applied by any manager regardless of his skill, that virtually no preparation is necessary for its use, and that it can spring full-blown into existence and transform industrial relationships overnight.

Some critics of participation, on the other hand, see it as a form of managerial abdication. It is a dangerous idea that will under-mine management prerogatives and almost certainly get out of control. It is a concept which for them fits the pattern of "soft" management exclusively. It wastes time, lowers efficiency, and weakens management's effectiveness.

A third group of managers view participation as a useful item in their bag of managerial tricks. It is for them a manipulative device for getting people to do what they want, under conditions which delude the "participators" into thinking they have had a voice in decision making. The idea is to handle them so skillfully that they come up with the answer which the manager had in the first place, but believing it was their own. This is a way of "making people feel important" which these managers are quick to empha-size as a significant motivational tool of management. (It is impor-tant to note the distinction between making people *feel* important and *making* people important.)

Naturally, there are severe critics of this manipulative approach to participation, and they tend to conceive of all participation as taking this form.

A fourth group of managers makes successful use of participa-tion, but they don't think of it as a panacea or magic formula. They do not share either the unrestrained enthusiasm of the fad-dists or the fears of the critics. They would flatly refuse to employ participation as a manipulative sales device.

Among all of these groups is a rather general but tacit agree-ment—incorrect, I believe—that participation applies to groups and not to individuals. None of them appears to view it as having any relationship to delegation. After all, it has a different name! Many of the strong proponents of delegation have no use whatever for participation.

In the light of all this it is not surprising that a fair number of thoughtful managers view this whole subject with some skepticism.

The effective use of participation is a consequence of a mana-gerial point of view which includes confidence in the potentialities of subordinates, awareness of management's dependency downwards, and a desire to avoid some of the negative consequences of emphasis on personal authority. It is consistent with Theory Y—with management by integration and self-control. It consists basically in creating opportunities under suitable conditions for people to influence decisions affecting them. That influence can vary from a little to a lot.

It is perhaps most useful to consider participation in terms of a range of managerial actions. At one end of the range the exercise of authority in the decision-making process is almost complete and participation is negligible. At the other end of the range the exercise of authority is relatively small and participation is maximum. There is no implication that more participation is better than less. The degree of participation which will be suitable depends upon a variety of factors, including the problem or issue, the attitudes and past experience of the subordinates, the manager's skill, and the point of view alluded to above.

Let us suppose that a manager has made a decision which will affect his subordinates. The circumstances are such that he feels that he cannot permit them to share in making this decision, but he is concerned to have them accept it with the best grace possible. He might hold a discussion in which he would inform them of the decision and reasons for it, and give them an opportunity to raise questions about it. His purpose would be to test the decision to see if it is acceptable. If he finds that it is strongly resented, he may be tempted to modify it rather than to risk the possibilities that it may be sabotaged. If it is not strongly resisted, his subordinates have at least had an opportunity to understand why he has made the decision and to clarify any aspects of it which are obscure. Such a discussion as this—when held under circumstances that permit genuine interaction—involves a limited degree of participation.

A slightly different situation might arise when a superior, having made a decision, would discuss with his subordinates the best way of implementing it. Often the implementation of a decision can occur in various ways, and it may make relatively little difference to the superior which of these alternatives is chosen, so long as the decision is carried out. The subordinates can have a voice in this matter which under some circumstances can be quite important to them. Such a situation involves somewhat more participation.

A third example involving still more participation would be the situation in which the superior discussed a pending decision with his subordinates before making it final. Under these conditions he would be ready to consider modifying his proposed decision or substituting another for it, depending upon the considerations which arose in discussion. The decision would still be his to make, but he would make it in the light of the discussion.

A still greater degree of participation would be involved if the superior were to present to his subordinates a problem facing him with the request that they help him find the best solution to it. He would not necessarily commit himself in advance to accepting any solution agreeable to them, but the understanding would be that if they could find a solution which he felt to be workable he would accept it.

Finally, there are some situations in which it is a matter of relative indifference to the superior which of several alternative decisions are made. These may be ones in which management has only a small stake and subordinates have a large one. Under these conditions the superior might say to his subordinates, "I will accept any decision which is agreeable to you."

Any of the above examples could occur at any level of an organization. Participation is not confined to the relationship between a first-line supervisor and his workers. It can occur between a president and his executive committee. Moreover, since there are many managerial decisions which affect a single subordinate, it is equally applicable to the individual or to the group. The kind of participation which will be utilized will vary depending upon the level of the organization as well as upon the other factors mentioned above.

The superior who is considering the use of participation will examine his strategy and the reasons for it in advance. If his subordinates are unaccustomed to having any influence on decisions affecting them, he will be unlikely to present a major issue to them on the first occasion, or to give them complete freedom of choice. He will be careful to indicate clearly the limits within which he is prepared to have them influence the decision. In making use of participation under these circumstances, he recognizes that he is beginning what may be a lengthy process of growth and learning for his subordinates, and for himself as well. He will plan to have them learn to crawl before they attempt to walk or run.

Since one of the major purposes of the use of participation is to encourage the growth of subordinates and their ability to accept responsibility, the superior will be concerned to pick appropriate problems or issues for discussion and decision. These will be matters of some significance to subordinates; otherwise they will see little point in their involvement. Some managers have limited their use of participation to subjects of so little concern to subordinates that there is no opportunity for growth. It may be fine to begin a participative approach at lower levels of the organization by asking employees to deal with such questions as car pools, United Fund drives, and the like. If the process stops here, however, the subordinates will soon recognize that management has no intention of permitting them to influence decisions of any moment, even though such decisions may have important consequences for them. The reaction then is likely to be a negative one to the whole

idea, and the managerial conclusion that employees are not interested in accepting responsibility will be entirely correct.

Of course, there are some risks connected with the use of participation. All significant managerial activities involve risk, and
this is no exception. The usual fear is that if employees are given
an opportunity to influence decisions affecting them, they will soon
want to participate in matters which should be none of their concern. Managements who express this fear most acutely tend to
have a very narrow conception of the issues which should concern
employees. If management's concern is with the growth of employees and their increasing ability to undertake responsibility,
there will of course be an expectation that employees will become
involved in an increasing range of decision-making activities.

As pointed out in Chapter 8, the experience in companies that
have acquired the point of view toward participation described
above—some of the Scanlon Plan companies, for example—has
not supported this fear. Perhaps the significant point is that management itself changes its attitude and becomes increasingly willing to have employees influence decisions of wider significance.
As mentioned earlier, the Scanlon company managers seem completely unable to comprehend the anxieties of others about the
loss of management prerogatives. They feel that they have full
control over the management of the business, and yet at the same
time they are quite willing to have employees discuss and influence
almost any managerial decision. Many non-Scanlon managers, on
the other hand, cannot conceive of such a situation except in terms
of a severe weakening of managerial control.

I am led to wonder what is cause and what is effect in this matter. Those managements who are most worried about their prerogatives seem, in general, to have the greatest difficulty in protect-
ing them. It is at least possible that this suspicious, almost para-
noid, attitude of management actually tends to *promote* interfer-
ence with management prerogatives, to create targets which em-

ployees promptly shoot at. The chain of events in some companies amounts to a self-fulfilling prophecy: Management expects certain things to happen, and it behaves in such a fashion that they do happen. Then management reverses cause and effect in its inter‑ pretation of what has taken place.

In any event, there are now so many instances of the successful use of participation which has not in any discernible way weakened management's ability to manage that I can see little basis for anxiety over the issue of management prerogatives. The only conclusion I would draw is that the managements who are primarily concerned to protect their power and authority had better leave the whole matter alone.

It is apparent that participation in the terms discussed above is quite consistent with the general theoretical approach of this whole volume. In view of the interdependence characteristic of industrial organizations there is reason for modifying the typical unilateral nature of the decision-making process. Participation, used judiciously, and in many different ways, depending upon the circumstances, offers help along these lines. It is a process which differs very little from delegation in its essential character. In fact, participation is a special case of delegation in which the subordinate gains greater control, greater freedom of choice, with respect to his own responsibility. The term participation is usually applied to the subordinate's greater influence over matters within the sphere of his superior's responsibilities. When these matters affect him and his job—when interdependence is involved—it seems reasonable that he should have the opportunity to exert some influence. Thus, for example, the target-setting approach discussed in Chapter 5 involves both delegation and participation. The ideas involved in these two concepts are not mutually exclusive but complementary.

Participation which grows out of the assumptions of Theory Y offers substantial opportunities for ego satisfaction for the subordinate and thus can affect motivation toward organizational objectives. It is an aid to achieving integration. In the first place, the subordinate can discover the satisfaction that comes from tackling problems and finding successful solutions for them. This is by no means a minor form of satisfaction. It is one of the reasons that the whole do-it-yourself movement has grown to such proportions in recent years. Beyond this there is a greater sense of independence and of achieving some control over one's destiny. Finally, there are the satisfactions that come by way of recognition from peers and superiors for having made a worth-while contribution to the solution of an organizational problem. At lower levels of the organization, where the opportunities for satisfactions like these are distinctly limited, participation in departmental problem solving may have considerable significance in demonstrating to people how they can satisfy their own needs best by working toward organizational objectives.

Viewed thus, participation is not a panacea, a manipulative device, a gimmick, or a threat. Used wisely, and with understanding, it is a natural concomitant of management by integration and self-control.

REFERENCES

Argyris, Chris, "Organizational Leadership and Participation in Management," *The Journal of Business,* vol. 28, no. 1, 1955.

Coch, Lester, and John R. P. French, Jr., "Overcoming Resistance to Change," *Human Relations,* vol. 1, no. 4, 1948, pp. 512–532.

Maier, Norman R. F., *Psychology in Industry,* 2d ed. New York: Houghton Mifflin Company, 1955.

Tannenbaum, Robert, and Warren H. Schmidt, "How to Choose a Leadership Pattern," *Harvard Business Review,* vol. 36, no. 2 (March–April), 1958.

10

The Managerial Climate

Theory X leads naturally to an emphasis on the tactics of control—to procedures and techniques for telling people what to do, for determining whether they are doing it, and for administering rewards and punishments. Since an underlying assumption is that people must be made to do what is necessary for the success of the enterprise, attention is naturally directed to the techniques of direction and control.

Theory Y, on the other hand, leads to a preoccupation with the *nature of relationships,* with the creation of an environment which will encourage commitment to organizational objectives and which will provide opportunities for the maximum exercise of initiative, ingenuity, and self-direction in achieving them.

Up to this point, we have been looking primarily at strategies and tactics of management—at methods of influence and control, target setting, performance appraisal, the administration of salaries and promotions, and the Scanlon Plan. Let us now turn to an examination of relationships and their significance.

In considering the psychological environment of people at work, one thinks first of the relationship between superior and subordinate. This relationship has been the subject of intensive research for several decades, and a good deal is known about it today.

As we have already seen, a central characteristic of this relationship is the interdependence of the parties. Since each of the parties in an interdependent relationship affects to some degree the other's ability to achieve his goals or satisfy his needs, major difficulties are likely to arise unless both have positive expectations that the relationship will further these purposes. Taking first the point of view of the subordinate, let us ask what determines his expectations?

A quick answer might be company policies and procedures, such as those that are usually described in a handbook for new employees. These are important, of course, but the correlation between the quality of the relationship and any particular set of personnel policies is relatively low. Companies having all the standard programs and practices may have excellent relations or very poor ones. Particular programs and practices in some companies may be a constant target for attack and a continuous source of friction. Essentially the same procedures in other companies may be completely accepted.

Since the subordinate is dependent on the superior, he is sensitive to a wide range of clues which influence his prediction of the success he will have in achieving his goals. More important than the existence of particular policies or the formal statements concerning them are evidences of how they are administered. The day-by-day behavior of the immediate superior and of other significant people in the managerial organization communicates something about their assumptions concerning management which is of fundamental significance.

The Climate of the Relationship

Many subtle behavioral manifestations of managerial attitude create what is often referred to as the psychological "climate" of the relationship. During childhood, when we were all in relationships involving extreme dependence, each of us acquired a high level of skill in perceiving aspects of parental behavior which told us whether everything was "all right" with the relationship. Even very small children are amazingly sensitive to quite unconscious manifestations of parental attitudes of acceptance or rejection. It is understandable that this should be so because of the extreme dependence of infancy and early childhood. In the psychological sense, survival is at stake.

Granted that the subordinate's dependence is far less in the employment relationship, it remains true that his ability to achieve his goals is materially affected by the attitudes of his superiors. He will make constant use of his ability to perceive the climate of the relationship in forming judgments about the opportunities for achieving his goals. The climate is more significant than the type of leadership or the personal "style" of the superior. The boss can be autocratic or democratic, warm and outgoing or remote and introverted, easy or tough, but these personal characteristics are of less significance than the deeper attitudes to which his subordinates respond.

The mechanical superintendent in a small manufacturing company was the prototype of the "bull of the woods" manager. He swore at his men, drove them, disciplined them, behaved superficially like a Napoleon. He was the despair of the staff group who were carrying on a program of supervisory training in human relations. Yet, oddly, his subordinates appeared to have high regard for him. They said, "Oh, his bark is worse than his bite." Morale and productivity in his department were both high.

Probing revealed some significant facts. He was known as a "square shooter" who dealt with his men with scrupulous fairness. Despite his superficial toughness he was sincerely and warmly interested in his subordinates. When they were in trouble—whether it was a simple matter of a few dollars to tide a man over until payday, or a family crisis—he helped out in a matter-of-fact way that left no uncomfortable feeling of being patronized.

Most important of all, he was known to be ready to go to bat for his men on any occasion when he felt they had not been accorded a fair break by higher management. The men spoke with awe of two occasions during a ten-year period when he had stormed into the office of the big boss to demand that a decision be altered because it was unfair to "his boys." When he was refused in one of these instances, he resigned on the spot, put on his hat, and left. His superior actually followed him out to the gate and capitulated.

While perhaps this man left something to be desired with respect to current conceptions of good management, he was, nevertheless, successful in developing and maintaining his subordinates' confidence in him. His managerial attitude cut across authoritarianism, permissiveness, paternalism, firmness and fairness, and all the other "styles" of management to create a deep and satisfying emotional certainty of fair treatment.

Confidence in a Fair Break

The research studies of the superior-subordinate relationship have pointed to a number of variables in the behavior and attitude of the superior which correlate both with high productivity and with the morale of subordinates. Many of these have to do with the subordinate's expectation that he will receive a fair break in attempting to achieve his own goals. The studies by the staff of the Institute for Social Research at the University of Michigan, for example, have stressed "employee-centered supervision." They find a positive correlation between this managerial attitude of genuine concern for the welfare of subordinates on the one hand and morale and productivity on the other.

This attitude, as the Michigan researchers have pointed out, is necessary but not sufficient. It is important also that the superior himself have influence upward in the organization. It is not enough for the subordinate to be liked by his superior, the latter must be able to do something about it. If the boss cannot carry substantial influence with respect to decisions on salary increases, promotion, or working conditions, his subordinates will have little confidence in him no matter what his attitude may be.

There is also the necessity for the boss to be competent—not that he is necessarily familiar with the details of every job under him, but that he is a capable manager. Subordinates cannot be confident that they will get a fair break from a manager who is incompetent.

It is sometimes thought that *security,* rather than the expectation of receiving the fairest possible break, is what is required. However, in these adult relationships it does not appear that the guarantees implied by the usual meaning of the term security are necessary. In fact, there are successful relationships—characterized by high morale and high productivity—in which security is literally zero. These conditions are found, for example, in certain military units on the battlefield.

Subordinates demand security when they feel threatened, when they fear arbitrary action, favoritism, discrimination. They ask only for a fair break when they have genuine confidence in their superiors.

An interesting illustration of this point occurred in a defense plant during World War II. The president of this company was absent on an assignment in Washington. The union, during the annual negotiations, demanded that the principle of plant-wide seniority be applied to all promotions within the worker ranks. The president, unwilling to take a strike, instructed his management to accede to this demand, and they did so.

The industrial relations staff of this company was persuaded that the fundamental reason for the intensity of the demand for seniority was a lack of confidence on the part of the workers in the way promotions were being administered. The workers believed—and with some justification—that many supervisors were playing favorites with liked and discriminating against disliked individuals.

The staff persuaded the management to undertake a series of actions designed to improve the leadership of supervision. These activities were carried on for about three years. There were indications that they were reasonably effective.

At the close of the war the president returned and prepared to carry on the union negotiations himself for the first postwar contract. The industrial relations manager suggested that since he was prepared to make substantial economic concessions, he might expect something in return. He urged the president to seek modifications in the seniority clause.

The president was unconvinced. His belief was that once a concession of this kind had been made it was next to impossible to withdraw it. Nevertheless, he was persuaded to make the attempt. When he did so, toward the close of the negotiations, he was considerably surprised to have the union agree, almost without argument. A new promotion clause was negotiated which gave merit 100 per cent of the weight in the determination of promotions. Seniority remained a factor along with merit only in the administration of layoffs. That clause, negotiated in 1946, remains in the union contract today.

A plausible interpretation of this situation is that the workers, threatened by the arbitrary and unfair administration of promotion policies, demanded the only form of protection that made sense to them: strict seniority (a purely objective measure which is not subject to personal judgment). However, when the conditions were altered so that these same workers had genuine confidence that they would receive a fair break from their bosses, they were quite willing to accept a policy in which this form of security was eliminated.

Confidence thus rests heavily on the subordinates' belief in the integrity of the superior, When one is dependent, any suspicion that the superior cannot be fully trusted arouses anxiety. It is obvious that neither techniques nor formulas, nor any particular leadership style, will *in themselves* fulfill this requirement. Techniques which are used as "gimmicks" can, on the other hand, readily destroy confidence.

The superior, for example, who utilizes "participation" as a manipulative device to trick subordinates into accepting his predetermined decisions or problem solutions runs a great risk of undermining their belief in his integrity. If his technique is recognized, as it likely will be, he will lose far more than he had hoped to gain by "making them feel important."

Another formula is that of displaying a "personal interest" in the worker. Some managers pride themselves on their skill in this technique, simply as a technique, when in fact their interest is negligible.

I remember accompanying a production manager through his plant some years ago and watching him show off his memory by his first-name greetings and questions about their families to several dozen workers. Despite its hearty quality, the whole performance had a ring of insincerity, but the verification of my suspicions came a week later when the plant voted by an overwhelming majority to be represented by a militant union, and I learned from the union organizer that a prime factor influencing the vote was the violent hostility toward this manager.

Confidence Downward

These characteristics of daily behavior and attitude to which subordinates respond with such sensitivity do not spring from the air. They are manifestations of the superior's conception of the managerial job and his assumptions about human nature. Consider a manager who holds people in relatively low esteem. He sees himself as a member of a small elite endowed with unusual capacities, and the bulk of the human race as rather limited. He believes also that most people are inherently lazy, prefer to be taken care of, desire strong leadership. He sees them as prepared to take advantage of the employment relationship unless they are closely controlled and firmly directed. In short, he holds to Theory X.

It is obvious that this theoretical orientation will reflect itself in a variety of ways in this manager's daily behavior toward his subordinates. It is equally obvious that, perceiving his attitudes, they will have relatively limited expectations concerning the possibilities for achieving their own goals in a relationship where they are dependent on him.

Over a period of several months, a group of workers in a manufacturing plant brought a lengthy series of grievances to management, all of them involving wages, working conditions, and plant rules. The intensity with which these grievances were pursued, and their frequency, led the personnel manager to suspect that they were symptoms of a deeper problem. He finally succeeded in creating a situation in which these employees felt free to express their private feelings, and it turned out that his hunch was indeed correct. The real issue had nothing to do with the actual subject of the grievances, but with the fact that the behavior of their supervisor made them feel he regarded them as "stupid lunks" and "dirt under his feet." They recognized that they could not get anywhere by raising grievances over the largely intangible characteristics of his behavior, so they expressed their violent reaction by making issues over tangible but irrelevant matters.

When the personnel manager discussed the whole question with the supervisor, he finally said, "I guess that's the way I do feel about them, but I can't imagine what I've done to show it. I knew it would make my job tougher, so I hid my feelings even when they were making trouble with all their grievances."

Consider now a manager with a contrasting set of attitudes. He has a relatively high opinion of the intelligence and capacity of the average human being. He may well be aware that he is endowed with substantial capacity, but he does not perceive himself as a member of a limited elite. He sees most human beings as having real capacity for growth and development, for the acceptance of responsibility, for creative accomplishment. He regards his subordinates as genuine assets in helping him fulfill his own responsibilities, and he is concerned with creating the conditions which enable him to realize these assets. He does not feel that people in general are stupid, lazy, irresponsible, dishonest, or antagonistic. He is aware that there are such individuals, but he expects to encounter them only rarely. In short, he holds to Theory Y.

The climate of the relationship created by such a manager will be vastly different. Among other things, he will probably practice effective delegation, thus providing his subordinates with opportunities to develop their own capabilities under his leadership. He will also utilize them as resources in helping him solve departmental problems. His use of participation will demonstrate his confidence in them.

Lawrence Appley, President of the American Management Association, once said that participation meant to him:

1. Analyzing a problem and arriving at the best solution he could find
2. Calling his subordinates together to discuss the problem
3. Leaving the meeting with a better solution than the one he began with

This comment indicates both the meaning of participation and the confidence in one's subordinates which is essential to its effective use.

Perhaps it is now clear that the all-important climate of the superior-subordinate relationship is determined not by policy and procedure, nor by the personal style of the superior, but by the subtle and frequently quite unconscious manifestations of his underlying conception of management and his assumptions about people in general. The most careful and well-conceived policies and procedures of personnel administration, the most elaborate training in the techniques of supervision, knowledge of all the tricks of winning friends and influencing people, will be interpreted by subordinates as manipulative and exploitative devices unless the climate is right. This is why the same policies and procedures yield different results in different organizations.

Who Determines the Climate?

The implication throughout this discussion has been that the superior in the interdependent superior-subordinate relationship is the one who really determines the quality of the relationship. It is reasonable to ask whether the subordinates' attitudes do not also have a great deal to do with the results. Of course they do. Personal attitudes, prejudices, and theoretical convictions about human beings aside, a superior cannot have confidence in a genuinely incompetent, or a dishonest, or a neurotically hostile subordinate. Moreover, some personalities are simply incompatible for reasons which neither party can do much about. Even with the best selection and placement procedures, managers sometimes face just such situations.

Under such conditions, it is nonsense to talk about creating positive expectations, mutual confidence, a healthy climate. The only real solution is to end the relationship, by transfer under some circumstances, or by termination of employment under others. If this is impossible, all that remains is to recognize that effective management in such a relationship is impossible, and to make the best of a bad situation.

Speaking generally of the superior-subordinate relationship, the dependence is greater upward than downward. This means that the superior exerts more control than the subordinate over the nature of the relationship. Sometimes situations which appear hopeless change when a new superior, because of his different attitudes, alters the psychological climate.

A few years ago I visited a large company where union-management relationships had been notoriously bad for a very long time until, about two years before my visit, they had changed dramatically for the better. The reason for my visit was that the company had been nominated by some officials of the international union and by citizens in the region as one deserving inclusion in a series of studies of constructive union-management relations.

The story related by the management of this company was so simple that it would have been unbelievable except for the evidence of its correctness. The company had been plagued by a violently hostile union. The local union leaders, elected by a minority of the membership who took the trouble to vote in the elections, were the worst "trouble-makers" in the company. Bargaining was a farce, grievances by the hundreds were pressed to the limit without regard for their merit, wildcat strikes were a regular phenomenon, restriction of production was widespread.

One influential member of top management persuaded his colleagues, after many heated discussions, to adopt a new approach. On the assumption that the bulk of the employees were decent human beings who would respond to reasonable treatment, the approach was to demonstrate in every possible way management's sincerity and integrity. The employee publications would no longer take a defensive position with respect to managerial practices. If a grievance hearing showed that management had been in the wrong, the error would be openly admitted and rectified immediately. Secrecy (motivated by fears of union misuse of information) would be replaced by complete openness and frankness. Extensive efforts would be made to help middle and lower management to understand and adopt this philosophy in their daily practice.

Within two years the whole relationship had become a different one as a result of this change in managerial strategy. Every one with whom I talked insisted there had been no other changed conditions which could explain what had happened. The former union leadership had been replaced by a group of highly respected, able individuals, grievances were down to a normal level, bargaining had been conducted in good faith and in an atmosphere of reasonableness, wildcat strikes had dropped to zero.

This management was still bemused and a little incredulous about what had happened. I could only think of Clinton Golden's sage comment that "By and large, and over the long run, management gets the kind of labor relations it deserves."

Underlying assumptions—theoretical considerations—influence managerial behavior not only with respect to policies and procedures and techniques, but with respect to subtle aspects of everyday behavior which determine the "climate" of human relationships. These daily manifestations of theory and attitude in turn affect the expectations of subordinates concerning their ability to achieve their goals and satisfy their needs through membership in the organization. Formal policies, programs, and procedures will be administered, and in turn perceived in the light of the managerial climate. Its importance is primary—the "machinery" of administration is secondary.

REFERENCES

Kahn, Robert, and Daniel Katz, "Leadership Practices in Relation to Productivity and Morale," in D. Cartwright and A. Zander, *Group Dynamics: Research and Theory.* Evanston, Ill.: Row, Peterson & Company, 1953.

Kahn, Robert L., Floyd C. Mann, and Stanley Seashore, "Human Relations Research in Large Organizations," *Journal of Social Issues,* vol. 12, nos. 1 and 2, 1956.

Kline, Bennet E., and Norman H. Martin, "Freedom, Authority and Decentralization," *Harvard Business Review,* vol. 36, no. 3 (May–June), 1958.

Leavitt, Harold J., "Small Groups in Large Organizations," *The Journal of Business,* vol. 28, no. 1, 1955.

Likert, Rensis, "Developing Patterns of Management," American Management Association, General Management Series, no. 182, 1956.

Pelz, Donald C., "Influence: A Key to Effective Leadership in the First-line Supervisor," *Personnel,* vol. 29, no. 3, 1952.

Walker, Charles R., Robert H. Guest, and Arthur N. Turner, *The Foreman on the Assembly Line.* Cambridge, Mass.: Harvard University Press. 1956.

11

Staff-Line Relationships

The importance of the climate of the superior-subordinate relationship is fairly well recognized today, and a good deal of attention is given to its creation and maintenance. Another interdependent relationship, however, has been less extensively studied, and the significance of its climate to the welfare of the enterprise is not so well understood. This is the relationship between staff and line.

Conventional organization theory deals with the staff-line relationship in terms of the principle of authority, naturally. The central chain of command is that of operations; other functions provide services and advice to the line. They cannot be given authority (except within their own functions) because to do so would violate the principle of unity of command: that any individual must have only one boss. There can, of course, be more than one line function (sales, for example), so long as there is sufficient independence that the principle of unity of command is not violated.

A second relevant principle is that authority must equal responsibility. Since the line requires certain services in fulfilling its responsibilities, it must have authority over them.

These principles may be given formal recognition in organization charts and position descriptions, but one would never deduce them from study of the realities of organizational life! Every member of lower and middle line management is subject to influences from staff groups which are psychologically indistinguishable from the authority exercised by his line superiors.

Such influences are not limited to people above the manager in the hierarchy either. A clerk in accounting may disallow an expense item in the budget of a general manager; a proposed salary increase initiated by a plant superintendent may require approval by a clerk in the personnel department. The fact that these staff people are following procedures formally approved by the line does not alter the psychological nature of the influence involved or the reactions to it.

In the textbooks on organization one finds elaborate circumlocutions designed to reconcile such inconsistencies. However, euphemistic terms like "coordination," "the authority of knowledge," and "acting in the name of" do not hide the fact that the conventional staff-line distinction in terms of authority is an illusion. The industrial organization is an elaborate complex of interdependent relationships, and interdependence means that each party can affect the ability of the other to achieve his goals and satisfy his needs. So long as the basic managerial strategy is one of direction and control, authoritative forms of influence exercised by staff groups will creep into the relationship no matter what the logical principles require. The struggle for power in a setting where goal achievement is based on acquiring it will not be eliminated by recourse to logic.

The climate of line-staff relationships in industry today does not often reflect the quality of mutual confidence described in Chapter 10. Quite typically, line managers regard staff groups as a "burden" rather than as a source of help. They see them as preoccupied with their narrow specialties to the point where they are unconcerned about the welfare of the business as a whole. They look on staff advice as generally impractical, usually hemmed in by overly standardized and bureaucratic procedures. As one line manager who was working out some difficult problems in union-management relations put it: "I keep away from the staff. They'd help me to death."

Staff groups, on the other hand, frequently have a jaundiced view of the line. They perceive line managers as exclusively concerned with maintaining their authority and independence, lacking in appreciation of the professional qualifications and accomplishments of staff groups, basically resistant to change and improvement.

These attitudes are often covered over by a quantity of humorous kidding, the hostility in which is barely concealed. There are exceptions, of course, but by and large staff-line relationships are far from ideal. In private conversation with either group, a casual comment about the other is often sufficient to start a torrent of deprecatory comment interspersed with "see if you can top this" illustrations. A term which frequently comes to minds is "scapegoating."

The Line Utilizes the Staff

There are many causal factors behind this rather unsatisfactory state of affairs. One of the most important is related, I believe, to line management's growing appreciation of the inadequacy of authority as the exclusive means of managerial control. However, the appreciation is at the level of practice rather than theory, and this is the source of much difficulty.

Too much reliance on authority produces counterforces among subordinates. Even the manager who is committed to the assumptions of Theory X becomes aware of this. Among the alternatives which have been offered as solutions to this problem is that of delegation. This principle, as ordinarily presented, emphasizes such ideas as "putting decisions near the point of action," controlling subordinates "through policy," giving "general rather than detailed supervision," and allowing subordinates "the freedom to make mistakes."

The upper-level manager who holds to Theory X can usually accept the idea of delegation, but when he puts it into action he is faced with a loss of the control on which his whole conception of management is based. He is helpless before the possibility that poor decisions may be made; productivity may drop, things may get out of hand. Since he lacks genuine confidence in his subordinates, these fears are real.

Fortunately, as he usually discovers, there is a way out of the dilemma. He can delegate and yet keep control. He need not rely on authority in the direct sense *if he can assign to someone else* the responsibility (1) for making sure his subordinates stay within policy limits and (2) for collecting and providing him with data which will enable him to know what is happening in time to step in before serious trouble arises.

Accordingly, he begins to use staff groups such as accounting, personnel, and engineering to develop and administer a system of managerial controls. When he adopts a policy, he assigns to the appropriate staff the responsibility for working out the necessary procedures and making sure they are followed. (After all, he has made the essential decision; let the specialists work out the details. Moreover, he can't spend his time worrying about whether specific procedures are followed; his concerns are with policy and with results. Let the staff "coordinate" the implementation.)

As a manager it is his responsibility to know what goes on. He can't abdicate, even if he delegates. If he can get daily reports on certain crucial aspects of the operation, and weekly and monthly reports on other aspects, he will be able with very little expenditure of time (and without breathing down anybody's neck in the old authoritarian way) to delegate without losing his ability to direct and control.

As a further refinement, he discovers the principle of "management by exception." It is not necessary to study a lot of detailed reports of the activities of his subordinates. The staff can do this for him, and prepare reports which point up only those things which are out of line and therefore require his attention. He may even go one step further and assign to the staff the task of investigating the "variances" and correcting them—reporting to him only those they are unable to handle themselves.

Now things are in good shape. He no longer exercises close, direct authority over his subordinates. He has delegated to them. He directs by means of policy; the decisions are made at the point of action; his subordinates have the freedom to make mistakes. There is no risk involved because he has a group of staff specialists who keep a detailed eye on every important aspect of the operations. He can concern himself with major problems, with formulating policy, with the more important aspects of management, because things are "under control." If anything is not as it should be, either the staff will see that it is corrected or notify him so that he can take care of it before serious difficulties arise.

A nice situation—or a travesty? It depends on your theoretical assumptions. There are textbooks, articles, and consulting firms which will provide help in setting up this kind of a managerial strategy, complete with control charts and colored signals. Of course, it will be necessary to reckon with some consequences. The staff have now become policemen, exercising by proxy the direct authority which was "relinquished" by the line. Countermeasures of a familiar kind will appear, but they will be directed toward the staff and, because the staff is neither particularly feared nor respected, the countermeasures may be even more effective than if they were directed at line management. There is a fair amount of research evidence indicating that middle and lower management groups tend to develop protective mechanisms which, although more elaborate and considerably more costly to the organization, are psychologically identical to those developed by workers to defeat the administration of individual incentive plans.

A large and successful manufacturing company discovered recently, after changing the management of a major division, what company top management described as "appalling" evidence of fudging of production and quality data, misreporting of costs, and ignoring of preventive maintenance which had been going on for years. The relevant headquarters staff groups, and even the division top staff people, were completely unaware of the situation until a new line management uncovered it.

The costs will not be trivial: subordinate managers will quickly develop their own independent data-gathering mechanisms (utilizing clerical time) to ensure that they will know at least as much as the staff about what is going on. Many man-hours will be consumed by the staff in tracking down variances which have already been discovered and corrected at the source. Ingenious methods for defeating staff control procedures will be developed, and the staff will be kept busy developing new ones to compensate for these. Antagonisms between line and staff will prevent the kind of collaboration that is essential for achieving organizational objectives. (Examples like those cited in Chapter 8 of the employees who "followed the blueprint" with glee when they knew that doing so would result in an unsatisfactory product will be multiplied many times over at various managerial levels.) Those controls which the superior indicates by his actions are important to him will be carefully watched by subordinates; others will be ignored. If such costs as these are worth the gains, this form of "delegation and control" will work after a fashion. Human beings are surprisingly adaptable. Basically, however, there are few managerial practices which produce as many negative consequences for the organization as this one of assigning control responsibilities to the staff. Whether my analysis of the reasons for it is correct or not, the practice (in varying degrees and forms) is widespread.

I believe these phenomena are responsible to a large degree for the "accordion effect" often noted in large companies. First, a big movement toward decentralization takes place. A few years later, after the consequences described above have taken their toll, top management decides that things have gotten out of hand, and there is a general tightening up in the direction of centralization. The inability to control a large, complex organization centrally leads after a while to a new attempt at decentralization. There are indications that this cycle has also occurred within Soviet industry, although the surface manifestations have been different.

The logic behind the strategy of control outlined above is so subtly persuasive that it is difficult to argue against it: Every manager is responsible for results within that portion of the organization which is under his supervision. He is held accountable by those above him. Obviously he cannot fulfill this responsibility unless (1) he knows what is going on within the unit, and (2) he is able to do something about things that go wrong.

This logic is unassailable if one accepts the assumptions of Theory X: that most people have to be made to do what is necessary for the success of the organization, that they will not voluntarily accept responsibility, that they are limited in capacity. Management by direction and control inevitably results in strategies similar to the one we have been examining.

The headquarters staff group in one large organization who are responsible for administering an elaborate control system throughout the company openly express the view that the only way to keep middle and lower management on their toes is to measure their performance constantly and in detail, and to "use the needle" unsparingly.

The assumptions of Theory Y, however, deny this conception of management and, therefore, the logic that flows from it. Human beings possess an internal "control mechanism" which can largely render ineffective any form of external control. This is true even of physical coercion under certain conditions. However, they will, under appropriate conditions, exercise *self*-direction and *self*-control in the service of objectives to which they are committed. Every parent learns these truths as his children develop to adulthood. He will not be able to control their behavior once they are grown. Unless he begins at some point to rely on their capacity for self-direction and self-control, he will be helpless as they approach maturity. His task, therefore, is to help them discover socially acceptable objectives to which they can give their commitment, and to reduce gradually his own external control as they learn to exercise self-control. In this manner the great majority of children do become responsible adult members of society.

The industrial manager is dealing with adults who are only partially dependent. They can—and will—exercise remarkable ingenuity in defeating the purposes of external controls which they resent. However, they can—and do—learn to exercise self-direction and self-control under appropriate conditions. His task is to help them discover objectives consistent both with organizational requirements and with their own personal goals, and to do so in ways which will encourage genuine commitment to these objectives. Beyond this, his task is to *help* them achieve those objectives: to act as teacher, consultant, colleague, and only rarely as authoritative boss. He will not help them if he attempts to keep direction and control in his own hands; he will only hamper their growth and encourage them to develop countermeasures against him. Nor will he help them achieve organizational objectives if he establishes a police force, reporting to him, who will assume part or all of the task of control. This may divert the resentment, but it will intensify the negative consequences.

He can help them only if he is prepared to relinquish control in the conventional sense, only if he has enough confidence in their willingness and ability to achieve organizational objectives that he can risk some poor judgments and some mistakes as a natural cost of their growth.

In the retailing field, particularly during the past few years, some shifts in managerial attitude have yielded experiences which are instructive. A number of mail-order houses and department stores have abolished elaborate control procedures built around customer-purchase returns. It has been found that the great majority of customers are sufficiently honest that it is substantially cheaper to replace a returned purchase without question than it is to maintain elaborate policing and investigating procedures. To be sure, some people are dishonest. The question, however, is whether it is cheaper to set up procedures for dealing with the bulk of honest people or to build procedures for dealing with the dishonest few. In this field at least, the data are clear: the former strategy is economically superior.

And the Staff?

Line management's inept utilization of staff groups is but one of several causes of unsatisfactory staff-line relationships. Another, of perhaps equal importance, is the conception which staff specialists tend to have of their own role. In spite of the much greater emphasis on the social sciences in the undergraduate curriculum today, the engineer or the accountant or the personnel specialist typically enters industry with little understanding of the difficult role he will be required to take if he is to become an effective member of a staff group. The focus in his education has been upon the content of his specialty and upon its methods and techniques. The complex problems involved in an organization's effective utilization of his specialized knowledge and skills have seldom even been touched upon. He is usually completely naïve about his professional relationships and roles.

His training, as a matter of fact, tends to make him unusually vulnerable. He has been taught to find "the best answer." He has great confidence in the objectivity of his scientific techniques. His natural expectation is that the solutions resulting from his application of these techniques will be immediately and gratefully accepted by the organization. Management by direction and control seems perfectly reasonable, with the modification that "the authority of knowledge" is for him final. No reasonable human being would challenge it.

He soon finds, of course, that many of his fellow members of the organization are not reasonable human beings. Not only are they less than properly impressed with him as a person; they frequently reject the objective results of his scientific studies or refuse to use his latest-model techniques.

It does not take him long to conclude that a lot of line managers are stupid, relatively unconcerned about the welfare of the organization, preoccupied with maintaining their authority and independence.

In this setting he is more than happy to accept an assignment to develop a system of measurements for the control of line management operations. If he is an accountant or an engineer, he is likely to put great store by standardization and well-worked-out procedures and rules. The coordinative function is his meat. Here is a way to minimize the subjective, unpredictable elements in human behavior and obtain the kind of direction and control which will really improve the effectiveness of the enterprise. Now he can make use of his training and his talents. And, finally (and uncon-

sciously), here is the way to get back at these so-and-so's who
have no appreciation or understanding of the values of his specialized field.

This is certainly not the universal state of affairs, but it is common enough to create widespread difficulties in line-staff relations.
Theory X is a congenial theory for a great many staff specialists. It
explains the organizational world as they perceive it. Management
by direction and control is a natural way of life, not only with
respect to their subordinates in the staff function, but with respect
to their relations with middle- and lower-level line management.

The Power of the Staff

The final irony of this whole situation is that it is the staff and
not the line which is beginning to represent the real power in the
modern industrial corporation. Quite apart from their inheritance
of the control function, staff groups are the ones who make it possible for management to solve the ever more intricate problems of
today's world—in the financial, technical, scientific, legislative, economic, and human fields. Their knowledge and training in their
specialties, their techniques for analyzing and solving problems are
absolutely essential to the success of the modern enterprise.

Consequently, we have an odd reversal of conventional organization theory: The line—the central and fundamental authoritative
chain of command—is becoming increasingly dependent upon a
considerable number of specialized staff groups. Simultaneously
the staff groups—the advisory and service groups who "cannot
exercise authority" because of the logical necessity for unity of
command—are becoming, both by virtue of the importance of
their knowledge and skill and because of management's delegation
to them of control and coordinative functions, the dominant, influential core of the organization. In one very large company, 70
per cent of the personnel above the second level of supervision
are staff, and the proportion is growing.

Indirectly perhaps, but definitely and increasingly, *the industrial organization of today is being run by the staff*. Their knowledge and techniques have a profound influence on major decisions, they design and administer procedures, and their control functions provide much of the direction and control of the human resources of the enterprise.

Alice's Wonderland was not such a strange place after all.

REFERENCES

Argyris, Chris, "Human Problems with Budgets," *Harvard Business Review*, vol. 31, no. 1 (January–February), 1953.

Dalton, Melville, *Men Who Manage*. New York: John Wiley & Sons, Inc., 1959.

Glover, J. G., and C. L. Maze, *Managerial Control*. New York: The Ronald Press, 1937.

Myers, Charles A., and John G. Turnbull, "Line and Staff in Industrial Relations," *Harvard Business Review*, vol. 34, no. 4 (July–August), 1956.

12

Improving Staff-Line Collaboration

The problem we face is that of creating a climate of mutual confidence around staff-line relationships which will encourage collaboration in the achievement of organizational objectives rather than guerilla warfare. The creation of that climate requires understanding by line and staff alike that many of their present attempts to influence behavior are like digging channels to get water to flow uphill. The needed changes simply cannot occur as long as the underlying assumptions are those of Theory X. As we have seen, even fruitful concepts like those of delegation and decentralization are warped completely out of shape when they are applied within this theoretical framework.

As far as the line is concerned, most of the changes in strategy implied by Theory Y and discussed elsewhere in this volume are relevant to relationships with staff. There are, however, two additional considerations which apply with special significance to this relationship. The first has to do with the traditional principle that authority must equal responsibility.

The Inequality of Authority and Responsibility

Once more, the logic is impeccable: An individual cannot legitimately be held responsible for things he cannot control. However, as we have seen, the assumption that he *can* control them through the use of authority is fallacious. We have seen what happens when the manager fails to recognize the interdependence involved in his relationships with his subordinates. Similar consequences ensue when the interdependence between staff and line is ignored.

It is admittedly awkward and frustrating to be responsible for accomplishing objectives under conditions in which one cannot control the relevant factors in the situation. It would be much nicer if reality were different. However, given the complex interdependencies of modern society, we are often in such situations. Parents—responsible to society for bringing up their children to be effective citizens—face many influences on their children which they cannot control except in a very limited sense (the formal educational system provides an obvious illustration). The leaders of our Federal government—responsible for maintaining peace with other nations—are similarly limited.

Industrial management is responsible to the stockholders for the economic success of the enterprise. However, it cannot *control* consumers' preferences or their attitudes toward saving money or buying goods; the general economic health of the nation; legislation in municipal, state, or Federal bodies; labor unions; or a host of other phenomena, including the behavior of subordinates within the organization. It can *influence* many of these determining variables; it cannot control them—especially in the narrow sense of exerting authority over them.

The realities of modern organizational life place the manager at any level of the organization in a position where he cannot control many things which affect the results for which he is responsible. It is foolish indeed to emphasize the logical idea that his authority must equal his responsibility. If he lacks confidence in his subordinates or in staff groups, if he expects indifference, antagonism, and lack of responsibility on their part, he is placed in a situation which is bound to create severe pressures on him. This unrealistic principle will encourage him to resort to the kinds of inappropriate methods of control described in previous chapters. It will also encourage him to attempt to exercise authority over staff groups and thus to create other problems.

The friction which is common between lower levels of line production management and the maintenance function is at least to some extent created by the production manager's frustration with his inability to exercise authority over those who maintain the equipment for which he is responsible. Yet, in my experience, the existence of this friction is independent of whether maintenance is established as staff (in which case the production foreman theoretically possesses the necessary authority) or as part of a separate line engineering department (in which case the production foreman has no authority over those who maintain his equipment). The few instances I have encountered of genuinely effective collaboration between these groups have included examples of *both* types of formal relationship.

The requirement that authority must equal responsibility is not only impossible to fulfill; it is logically unnecessary *except within a system which makes authority the exclusive means of influence.* The first prerequisite for improving staff-line relationships is that we abandon this supposed requirement, and with it the corollary that the line exercises authority over the staff. The two groups are interdependent, and exclusive reliance on authority in this relationship is as inappropriate as it is in the superior-subordinate relationship.

Naturally, another casualty will be the practice on the part of any level of line management of assigning responsibilities to staff groups which entail their exercising authority (whether disguised by terms like "coordination" or "management by exception" or not) over lower levels of the organization. Let us see what this means in practice.

The Principle of Self-Control

The manager's utilization of staff groups within the context of Theory Y will emphasize the principle of self-control. He will perceive the staff as a resource for the whole organization; consequently he will not seek help from staff groups in any way which simultaneously threatens his subordinates (as is the case if he uses them as policemen).

With respect to data and reports compiled by staff groups, the principle of self-control requires that they be provided to each member of management for controlling *his own,* not his subordinates' jobs. Delegation means that he will concern himself with the *results* of their activities and not with the details of their day-to-day performance. This requires a degree of confidence in them which enables him to accept certain risks. Unless he takes these risks there will be no delegation.

Every manager is entitled to all the detailed data he wishes for purposes of self-control. If, however, the data are broken down in a fashion which reveals the day-to-day performance of individual subordinates, they are no longer data for self-control. His use of such information vitiates the idea of delegation completely. (The same thing is true, of course, if he assigns to staff the responsibility of "controlling" his subordinates by this means.)

This is a radical conception. It means, for example, that the manager of a division will have available to him data about the *division,* but not about the individual functions and departments within it. He may wish data about the division as a whole on a daily basis; he may wish a few general figures, or he may desire information on many aspects of divisional performance. His own preferences govern so long as he does not request details about the performance of individual subordinates. His subordinates in turn will operate in the same way, each reviewing whatever information he deems important to control his own, but not his subordinates', jobs.

If such summary data indicate to the manager that something is wrong within the organizational unit for which he is responsible, he will turn not to staff, but to his subordinates for help in analyzing the problem and correcting it. He will not assign staff "policemen" the task of locating the "culprit." If his subordinates have data for controlling their own jobs, the likelihood is that they will already have spotted and either corrected the difficulty themselves or sought help in doing so.

Procedures such as these will probably strike most managers as absurdly restrictive. They are stated this way in order to make perfectly clear the implications of the concept of self-control. Practically they may be accepted as ideals rather than formal requirements.

Self-control is a relative, not an absolute, concept. There may be more or less of it, depending upon a variety of circumstances. A subordinate who is new on the job is obviously not in a position to accept the responsibility for complete self-control. He and his superior might therefore agree to discuss the detailed data concerning his performance at frequent intervals. When some phase of organizational performance is temporarily given a critical importance, there may be the necessity for reducing the normal degree of self-control. A superior might, under such conditions, have an agreement with his subordinates that they would discuss with him immediately any important variances with respect to this variable.

The manager who understands the principle of self-control and is committed to it will adjust his tactics in many ways to meet the circumstances. Moreover, his subordinates will be fully aware of what he is doing and why. Knowing his commitment to the principle, they will accept the realistic necessities with little difficulty. In fact, when there is adequate understanding and commitment, it is of little consequence what data any manager receives. The problem is in the administrative misuse of such data by managers (line or staff) who either do not understand the implications of self-control or lack commitment to it. It takes but little observation to indicate how widespread these misuses are today. An important contributing factor is the almost complete lack of concern with the implications of self-control in the literature on managerial controls.

Managers frequently complain to me about the fact that subordinates "nowadays" won't take responsibility. They say, "I delegate, but they don't want the responsibility." I have been interested to note how often these same managers keep a constant surveillance over the day-to-day performance of subordinates, sometimes two or three levels below themselves.

The fundamental point, and the second prerequisite for improving staff-line relationships, is that management by integration and self-control involves the assumption that the subordinate can be helped to accept responsibility for his job and that he—not his superior or his superior's superior—should have the data he needs to control it.

One of the major fruits of industry's growing use of staff specialists during the past couple of decades has been the development of an elaborate "information technology." We have today methods of measurement and data collection and analysis which would have been inconceivable a quarter of a century ago. These developments are tremendously powerful. Moreover, the future holds the promise of even more spectacular growth.

The tragedy is the way in which the power provided by this increase in knowledge is being misused. We are defeating the very purposes which it would enable us to achieve, primarily because of a failure to examine our underlying assumptions. "Control" seems superficially to be a straightforward and practical concept, when in fact it is an exceedingly complex one.

The strategy of control implied by Theory Y places the staff in a very different role than the one it now occupies. This changed role (which would involve different expectations on the part of line and staff alike) represents a crucial requirement for creating a climate of mutual confidence in which the two groups can collaborate effectively to achieve the objectives of enterprise.

The Appropriate Role of Staff

The appropriate role of any major staff group (excluding a few, like an economic forecasting department, whose relationships are relatively limited) is that of providing professional help *to all levels of management*. In some cases, such as engineering, the help is provided primarily to one or two functions, e.g., manufacturing and sales. In other cases, such as accounting and personnel, the help is provided to all other functions.

The hierarchical nature of the organization has tended to focus attention on help given to the level at which the staff group reports. Rewards and punishments for staff members come from there. Moreover, prestige and status are greater the higher the level of "attachment." In large companies, where there are both headquarters and field staff groups, it is particularly important that the headquarters groups recognize and accept their responsibilities for providing help to *all* levels of management.

The provision of professional help is a subtle and complex process. Perhaps the most critical point—and the one hardest to keep clearly in mind—is that help is always defined by the recipient. Taking an action with respect to someone because "it is best for him," or because "it is for the good of the organization," may be influencing him, but it is not providing help *unless he so perceives it*. Headquarters staff groups tend to rationalize the effects of many of their activities on the field organization in a paternalistic manner and, as a consequence, fail to see that they are relying on inappropriate methods of control. When the influence is unsuccessful, the usual reaction occurs: The recipients of the "help" are seen as resistant, stupid, indifferent to organizational needs, etc. The provision of help, like any other form of control or influence, requires selective adaptation to natural law. One important characteristic of "natural law" in this case is that help is defined by the recipient.

The concept of management by direction and control carries the implication that staff groups reporting to a given manager will do what he tells them to. If he assigns a responsibility to a staff group which provides help to him, but at the same time hampers the effective performance of lower levels of management, this is his prerogative. If he places a staff group in the untenable position of being both policemen and "helpers," this is his affair. The duty of the staff group is to follow his orders.

This presents a difficult problem. An independent professional—be he lawyer, doctor, or industrial consultant—faced with such demands would raise the point of conflicting obligations. His professional ethics will not permit him to undertake to help one client at the expense of another. Moreover, his clients usually recognize the potentiality of negative consequences for themselves and agree.

An internal professional staff specialist faces the necessity of persuading those to whom he reports that they will defeat their own purposes if they do not abstain from creating conflicting obligations. The problem is not an ethical one alone. As we saw in connection with the problem of managerial controls in the previous chapter, it is a problem of ineffective as opposed to effective methods of achieving objectives. In this respect, staff groups face the necessity of undertaking an educational role relative to their superiors—a somewhat unusual but not unheard of relationship! In fact, this role is a major one for staff in a number of respects.

Let us examine briefly four kinds of help which the typical staff group will find itself called upon to provide. With respect to all of them, a primary consideration is that help is defined by the recipient.

1. *Help in Strategy Planning.* The specialized knowledge and skill in the use of the techniques of problem analysis and research possessed by staff groups are increasingly utilized by management, particularly at upper levels, in planning. Often the research and knowledge of a staff group will be the major determinant of organization policy or of managerial strategy.

The role of the staff in providing such help may be compared to the role of an architect in helping a client plan a new home. (The analogy cannot be pressed too far because the architect's role during actual construction is typically *not* comparable to the staff role after a managerial strategy has been decided.) The client has ideas concerning the kind of house he wants, and lots of experience in living. The architect has professional knowledge which can help the client to end up with a house which will better serve his needs than one which he might design for himself. The problem faced by the architect is to bring about an integration of his own and his client's ideas which will satisfy the client and at the same time utilize his own professional competence.

The client's original idea of the house he wants may be quite naïve, perhaps impractical, sometimes unnecessarily expensive. However, if the architect takes a condescending, or an authoritarian, position with respect to the client's ideas, he may find himself out of a job (unless his prestige is so high that the client will accept him on any terms). On the other hand, if the architect simply accepts the client's initial ideas, regardless of their merit, he is not serving the purpose for which he was hired. Given a relationship of mutual confidence, and skill in the consultant role as well as professional knowledge on the part of the architect, the necessary integration may be achieved.

Staff groups helping management in strategy planning have a similar role to occupy. If they are not sensitive to management's needs—expressed and unexpressed—their professional knowledge will not be utilized. On the other hand, if they attempt slavishly to give management what it requests, without bringing to bear their own professional knowledge, they are not fulfilling their responsibilities either to management or to the organization as a whole.

A colleague in the personal department of a manufacturing company was approached by several middle managers of a technical department who wanted a rapid reading course provided for their subordinates. Their diagnosis: The subordinates could not cope with the materials that piled up on their desks because they had insufficient reading skill. My colleague persuaded these managers to discuss the problem further with him. In the course of the discussion, they decided that it would be worth while to undertake a more detailed analysis of the situation, and they carried it out with his help. The findings: The heart of the problem lay, not in reading skill, but in job assignments, erroneous beliefs of the subordinates about what was expected of them, and other aspects of *the relationship between these managers and their subordinates*. Reading skill was a trivial factor.

The "clients" not only abandoned their original diagnosis and prescription; they involved my colleague as a helper in a rather complete reorganization of their department and a program focused on improving *their own* managerial competence.

While some staff groups—an economics department is a good example—devote their primary effort to strategy planning with upper-level management, others provide much less of this kind of professional help than they might. Many staff groups, for example, become so preoccupied with administering plans and programs and "putting out fires" that they do not fulfill this particular responsibility adequately. Others are unwilling to take the risks involved in attempting to persuade management that its diagnoses and prescriptions, in the absence of professional staff help, are often inadequate. Actually, much can be accomplished in top management education through competent professional help in strategy planning. Here the architect-client analogy is particularly relevant. Some of the recent talk, for example, about the "bankruptcy" of personnel administration may be significant in just this respect.

2. *Help in Problem Solving.* This form of professional help is not unlike that involved in strategy planning except that (1) it is likely to be concerned with more immediate and specific problems, and (2) it is provided to all levels of the organization. Exactly the same role is called for.

The danger with respect to this kind of professional help (in contrast to strategy planning with top management) is that staff groups too easily forget in their dealings with middle and lower management that help is defined by the recipient. It is one of the favorite pastimes of headquarters groups to decide from within their professional ivory tower what help the field organization needs and to design and develop programs for meeting these "needs." Then it becomes necessary to get field management to accept the help provided, and a different role is taken by the staff: that of persuading middle and lower management to utilize the programs. The term "selling" is often used to describe this process, but the power of headquarters staff groups (by virtue of their direct access to top management) is such that field management usually perceives the process as one of "buy or else." Field visits of headquarters staff members are often devoted almost exclusively to such selling of headquarters-designed programs or to checking up to see whether the field is using them.

This kind of help is one reason why the term "burden" is so often applied to staff groups. It is why my young friend referred to earlier feared that the staff would help him to death. It is why many staff-conceived programs which are "bought" by top management achieve indifferent success in the field.

If the staff is genuinely concerned with providing professional help to all levels of management it will devote a great deal of time to exploring "client" needs directly, and to helping the client find solutions which satisfy him. Often the most effective strategy for this purpose is one in which the client develops his own solution with professional help. As indicated by the rapid reading example in the previous section, helping the client diagnose his problem may often be a critical step in this strategy.

Problem-solving help to all levels of management, competently and sensitively provided, is *the* way to develop line confidence in the staff. The needed skills and the understanding of what is involved in providing this kind of help are all too rare among staff specialists today. Professional education in some fields is beginning to include training along these lines, but the need appears not even to be recognized in most engineering schools or schools of business.

In providing this kind of help, the professional specialist will sometimes face the problem of conflicting interests.

A personnel staff member, for example, may be asked by management to give a judgment on the qualifications or performance of a "client" at some lower level of the organization. Or he may, in the course of his professional work, become persuaded that a particular manager is doing substantial harm to the organization through lack of qualifications for his job.

He will destroy the possibility of providing professional help to all levels of management if he permits himself to be used as a source of information or judgment in such situations as these. In the latter case, direct discussion with the individual himself may be called for. However, if the staff man fulfills his responsibility to the organization by revealing his judgments about members of management to their superiors, he will soon preclude the possibility of fulfilling his responsibility for providing help to all levels of management. He cannot help one member of management at the expense of another, nor can he occupy successfully both the role of judge and the role of professional vis-à-vis his "clients."

There probably are cases where the staff member must compromise with respect to such conflicting obligations, but these will be extremely rare. The problem today, all too often, is that no consideration is given to this crucial aspect of the helping role. The consequences for the climate of staff-line relations are readily observable.

3. *Help with Respect to Managerial Controls.* This form of help has already been considered at some length, and it is perhaps now clear why conventional practice creates so many and such difficult problems. As indicated earlier, the principle of self-control requires that a staff group should never be asked to provide any manager with information to be used for the control of others. Granted that this is a theoretical requirement to which certain practical adjustments must be made, its significance should be very clearly understood by the staff. Otherwise, staff "help" will compound the problems discussed above.

The same principle—that staff provides help for self-control only—applies to what is usually called "coordination," but which means policing the organization with respect to policy and procedures. Help can consist in informing an individual that he is out of line, or that a contemplated action would be in violation of policy—*but with the full understanding by both parties that the staff member will not report his knowledge or opinion to anyone else.*

The helping role and the role of policeman are absolutely incompatible roles. To place an individual in the latter is to destroy the possibility of his occupying the former one successfully.

One further consideration with respect to the staff and controls deserves mention, and that is that maximum standardization is not necessarily accompanied by maximum efficiency. These two variables are less highly correlated than many professional specialists believe. In fact, there is a good deal to be said for establishing the goal of the *minimum* standardization of human behavior consistent with the ability to operate the organization. This idea quickly runs afoul of the aims and practices of those working in the data processing field in particular. The essential point, however, is that the decision which achieves organizational objectives must be *both* (1) technically and scientifically sound and (2) carried out by people. If we lose sight of the second of these requirements, or if we assume naïvely that people can be made to carry out whatever decisions are technically sound, we run a genuine risk of decreasing rather than increasing the effectiveness of the organization.

Top management in a large, geographically decentralized company became concerned over the size of their permanent inventory of replacement parts. The dollar figure was staggering. Accordingly, a consulting firm was hired to design and install an efficient purchase and inventory control system. The desired objective was to cut the investment in parts inventory in half.

The system designed by this firm was a marvel of efficiency. It included several volumes of coded parts listings and procedures, and a sizable staff to administer the program. A year after it was installed, the inventory investment had been reduced to the desired figure.

During a series of discussions with middle- and lower-level field management about this time, I was simply overwhelmed by the vehement condemnation of this system and of the way it was being administered. Examples, literally by the dozens, were cited of sizable but unnecessary costs to the organization which were resulting. Gross inefficiencies of many kinds were made necessary by rules and procedures which took too little account of local conditions and which provided almost no opportunity for the exercise of managerial judgment.

Of course, many of these managers disliked the curtailment of their freedom and the tightening up of free and easy practices. But the kinds of examples that were cited made it clear that much more than this was involved. The attitude was frequently expressed that "if top management doesn't care any more about waste and inefficiency than this, why should we." Many competent, sincere men said, in one form or another, "We have been wasteful sometimes, but we sure had an interest in the company's welfare. We could have shown them many ways to reduce the parts inventory that would still have permitted us to operate efficiently. But now we are completely hemmed in, and we find we can't do anything to change these unworkable rules. The headquarters staff won't listen. So we live with the rules, and we find ways —sometimes costly—to get around them. *And we're beginning not to give a damn whether the company loses or gains.*"

When I reported these field reactions to top management, they were dismissed as "typical gripes of guys whose sloppy practices have been corrected." The system of control had been designed by a good company; it cost a lot of money to install; the results in terms of the inventory figure were just what had been desired. And that was that.

4. *Help in Administering Services.* A fourth activity of staff groups is essentially a line operating function. It consists of administering certain services: equipment maintenance, plant security, payroll administration, eating facilities, activities made necessary by legislation, data processing facilities, benefit plans, etc. Often these requre more in the way of managerial than specialized professional skill, but they fall logically within the fields of competence of given staff groups, so they are left there to be administered.

There are no particular problems of staff-line relationships involved in this form of help except (1) poor administration when it occurs and (2) the problem just mentioned of the staff tendency to equate degree of standardization of practice with efficiency. There is a danger, as previously indicated, that staff groups may become so preoccupied with these administrative responsibilities that they fail to provide the degree and kind of professional help that the organization requires. If the incumbents of staff jobs are former line managers, or technically but not professionally trained specialists, they are likely to find these activities highly congenial. If, however, staff departments include a preponderance of trained and sophisticated professional specialists, there is little danger that the administrative tasks will have priority over genuinely professional activities—unless line management establishes such a priority by its assignment of responsibilities to the staff.

Summary

In order to create a climate of mutual confidence surrounding staff-line relationships within which collaboration in achieving organizational objectives will become possible, several requirements must be met:

1. The inadequacy of the conventional principles of unity of command and of equality of authority and responsibility must be recognized. Not only are these principles unrealistic in the modern industrial corporation, they are the source of many of the difficulties we are trying to correct. They are logically necessary within the context of Theory X, but flatly contradictory to Theory Y.
2. The primary task of any staff group is that of providing specialized help to *all levels* of management, not just to the level at which the group reports.

3. The proper role of the staff member is that of the professional vis-à-vis his clients. The genuinely competent professional recognizes (*a*) that help is always defined by the recipient and (*b*) that he can neither fulfill his responsibilities to the organization nor maintain proper ethical standards of conduct if he is placed in a position which involves conflicting obligations to his managerial "clients."

4. The central principle of managerial control is the principle of self-control. This principle severely limits *both* staff and line use of data and information collected for control purposes as well as the so-called coordinative activities of staff groups. If the principle of self-control is violated, the staff inevitably becomes involved in conflicting obligations, and in addition is required to occupy the incompatible roles of professional helper and policeman.

It may seem impractical to attempt to create a climate of staff-line relationships within the organization similar to that which characterizes effective professional-client relationships in private practice, yet this is essentially what is required. It becomes a possibility only within the context of Theory Y.

In Conclusion

We are now in a position to consider a couple of interesting questions about the staff-line relationship. First, where is the issue of who exercises authority over whom?

With the approach suggested above, the traditional principles which define the role of staff evaporate. The professional-client relationship is an interdependent one in which neither typically exercises authority over the other although there is influence in both directions. The managerial client is dependent on the specialized knowledge and skill of the professional, but if he attempts to get the help he needs by authoritative methods he will defeat his purposes. It is not possible to obtain by command the imaginative, creative effort which distinguishes the competent professional from the glorified clerk. The manager who perceives staff members as flunkies to carry out his orders will never obtain *professional* staff help. On the other hand, the manager who perceives himself as a client utilizing the knowledge and skill of professional specialists will not attempt to achieve this purpose by relying on his authority over them.

The professional, in turn, is dependent upon his clients. Unless they accept and use his help, he has no value to the organization and therefore there is no reason for employing him. If, however, he attempts to impose "help" authoritatively (whether directly or by accepting assignments of control and coordinative responsibilities from his superiors), he places himself in the role of policeman, which is completely incompatible with the professional role.

There is, in fact, no solution to the problem of staff-line relationships in authoritative terms which will achieve organizational objectives adequately. Waste of human resources, friction and antagonism, elaborate and costly protective mechanisms, and lowered commitment to organizational objectives are the inescapable consequences of the traditional conception of the relationship.

Second, what has happened to the distinction between line and staff? It has become evident as a result of our examination of line management's task in the preceding chapters of this volume that the most appropriate roles of the manager vis-à-vis his subordinates are those of teacher, professional helper, colleague, consultant. Only to a limited degree will he assume the role of authoritative boss. The line manager who seeks to operate within the context of Theory Y will establish relationships with his subordinates, his superiors, and his colleagues which are much like those of the professional vis-à-vis his clients. He will become more like a professional staff member (although in general rather than specialized ways) and less like a traditional line manager.

The various functions within the organization differ in many ways (in the number of other functions with which they are related, for example), but not particularly in terms of the traditional line-staff distinction. All managers, whether line or staff, have responsibilities for collaborating with other members of the organization in achieving organizational objectives. Each is concerned with (1) making his own resources of knowledge, skill, and experience available to others; (2) obtaining help from others in fulfilling his own responsibilities; and (3) controlling his own job. Each has *both* line and staff responsibilities.

One consequence of this approach is the greater significance which the managerial *team* acquires at each level of organization. Much of the manager's work—be he line or staff—requires his collaboration with other managers in a relationship where personal authority and power must be subordinated to the requirements of the *task* if the organizational objectives are to be achieved. Effective collaboration of this kind is hindered, not helped, by the traditional distinctions between line and staff. The goal is to utilize the contributions of all the available human resources in reaching the best decisions or problem solutions or action strategies.

The modern industrial organization is a vast complex of interdependent relationships, up, down, across, and even "diagonally." In fact, the interdependence is so great that only collaborative team efforts can make the system work effectively. It is probable that one day we shall begin to draw organization charts as a series of linked groups rather than as a hierarchical structure of individual "reporting" relationships. These points will be considered further in Chapter 16.

REFERENCES

Baumgartel, Howard, "Leadership, Motivations, and Attitudes in Research Laboratories," *Journal of Social Issues,* vol. 12, no. 2, 1956.

Bursk, Edward C., *The Management Team.* Cambridge, Mass.: Harvard University Press, 1954.

Leavitt, Harold J., and Thomas L. Whisler, "Management in the 1980's," *Harvard Business Review,* vol. 36, no. 6 (November–December), 1958.

Lippitt, Ronald, Jeanne Watson, and Bruce Westley, *Dynamics of Planned Change.* New York: Harcourt, Brace and Company, Inc., 1958.

McGregor, Douglas, "The Staff Function in Human Relations," *Journal of Social Issues,* vol. 4, no. 3, 1948.

Pelz, Donald C., "Motivation of the Engineering and Research Specialist," American Management Association, General Management Series, no. 186, 1957.

Sampson, Robert C., *The Staff Role in Management.* New York: Harper & Brothers, 1955.

Shepard, Herbert A., "Supervisors and Subordinates in Research," *The Journal of Business,* vol. 29, no. 4, 1956.

PART THREE: THE DEVELOPMENT OF MANAGERIAL TALENT

13

An Analysis of Leadership

Are successful managers born or "made"? Does success as a manager rest on the possession of a certain core of abilities and traits,
or are there many combinations of characteristics which can result
in successful industrial leadership? Is managerial leadership—or
its potential—a property of the individual, or is it a term for describing a relationship between people? Will the managerial job
twenty years from now require the same basic abilities and personality traits as it does today?

The previous chapters of this volume suggest tentative answers
to these questions. Knowledge gained from research in the social
sciences sheds additional light on these and other questions relevant to leadership in industry. It does not provide final, definitive
answers. There is much yet to be learned. But the accumulated
evidence points with high probability toward certain ones among a
number of possible assumptions.

Prior to the 1930s it was widely believed that leadership was a
property of the individual, that a limited number of people were

uniquely endowed with abilities and traits which made it possible for them to become leaders. Moreover, these abilities and traits were believed to be inherited rather than acquired.

As a consequence of these beliefs, research studies in this field were directed toward the identification of the universal characteristics of leadership so that potential leaders might be more readily identified. A large number of studies were published—many based on armchair theorizing, but some utilizing biographical or other empirical data.

Examinations of this literature reveals an imposing number of supposedly essential characteristics of the successful leader—over a hundred, in fact, even after elimination of obvious duplication and overlap of terms. The search still continues in some quarters. Every few months a new list appears based on the latest analysis. And each new list differs in some respects from the earlier ones.

However, social science research in this field since the 1930s has taken new directions. Some social scientists have become interested in studying the behavior as well as the personal characteristics of leaders. As a result, some quite different ideas about the nature of leadership have emerged.

The research in this field in the last twenty years has been prolific. A recent summary cites 111 references, of which six were published prior to 1930. As a result of such work, a number of generalizations about leadership may be stated with reasonable certainty. Among these, the following are particularly significant for management.

Generalizations from Recent Research

It is quite unlikely that there is a single basic pattern of abilities and personality traits characteristic of all leaders. The personality characteristics of the leader are not unimportant, but those which are essential differ considerably depending upon the circumstances. The requirements for successful political leadership are different from those for industrial management or military or educational leadership. Failure is as frequent as success in transfers of leaders from one type of social institution to another. The reasons are perhaps evident in the light of the discussion in earlier chapters of this volume.

Even within a single institution such as industry, different circumstances require different leadership characteristics. Comparisons of successful industrial leaders in different historical periods, in different cultures, in different industries, or even in different companies have made this fairly obvious. The leadership requirements of a young, struggling company, for example, are quite different from those of a large, well-established firm.

Within the individual company different functions (sales, finance, production) demand rather different abilities and skills of leadership. Managers who are successful in one function are sometimes, but by no means always, successful in another. The same is true of leadership at different organizational levels. Every successful foreman would not make a successful president (or vice versa!). Yet each may be an effective leader.

On the other hand, leaders who differ notably in abilities and traits are sometimes equally successful when they succeed each other in a given situation. Within rather wide limits, weaknesses in certain characteristics can be compensated by strength in others. This is particularly evident in partnerships and executive teams in which leadership functions are, in fact, *shared*. The very idea of the team implies different and supplementary patterns of abilities among the members.

Many characteristics which have been alleged to be essential to the leader turn out not to differentiate the successful leader from unsuccessful ones. In fact, some of these—integrity, ambition, judgment, for example—are to be found not merely in the leader, but in any successful member of an organization.

Finally, among the characteristics essential for leadership are skills and attitudes which can be acquired or modified extensively through learning. These include competence in planning and initiating action, in problem solving, in keeping communication channels open and functioning effectively, in accepting responsibility, and in the skills of social interaction. Such skills are not inherited, nor is their acquisition dependent on the possession of any unique pattern of inborn characteristics.

It is, of course, true that the few outstanding leaders in any field have been unusually gifted people, but these preeminent leaders differ widely among themselves in their strengths and weaknesses. They do not possess a pattern of leadership characteristics in common. The evidence to date does not prove conclusively that there is no basic universal core of personal qualifications for leadership. However, few of the social scientists who have worked extensively during recent years in this field would regard this as a promising possibility for further work. On the contrary, the research during the past two decades has shown that we must look beyond the personal qualifications of the leader if we wish to understand what leadership is.

Leadership Is a Relationship

There are at least four major variables now known to be involved in leadership: (1) the characteristics of the leader; (2) the attitudes, needs, and other personal characteristics of the followers; (3) characteristics of the organization, such as its purpose, its structure, the nature of the tasks to be performed; and (4) the social, economic, and political milieu. The personal characteristics required for effective performance as a leader vary, depending on the other factors.

This is an important research finding. *It means that leadership is not a property of the individual, but a complex relationship among these variables.* The old argument over whether the leader makes history or history makes the leader is resolved by this conception. Both assertions are true within limits.

The relationship between the leader and the situation is essentially circular. Organization structure and policy, for example, are established by top management. Once established, they set limits on the leadership patterns which will be acceptable within the company. However, influences from above (a change in top management with an accompanying change in philosophy), from below (following recognition of a union and adjustment to collective bargaining, for example), or from outside (social legislation, changes in the market, etc.) bring about changes in these organizational characteristics. Some of these may lead to a redefinition of acceptable leadership patterns. The changes which occurred in the leadership of the Ford Motor Company after Henry Ford I retired provide a dramatic illustration.

The same thing is true of the influence of the broader milieu. The social values, the economic and political conditions, the general standard of living, the level of education of the population, and other factors characteristic of the late 1800s had much to do with the kinds of people who were successful as industrial leaders during that era. Those men in turn helped to shape the nature of the industrial environment. Their influence affected the character of our society profoundly.

Today, industry requires a very different type of industrial leader than it did in 1900. Similarly, today's leaders are helping to shape industrial organizations which tomorrow will require people quite different from themselves in key positions.

An important point with respect to these situational influences on leadership is that they operate selectively—in subtle and unnoticed as well as in obvious ways—to reward conformity with acceptable patterns of behavior and to punish deviance from these. The differing situations from company to company, and from unit to unit within a company, each have their selective consequences. The observable managerial "types" in certain companies are illustrative of this phenomenon. One consequence of this selectivity is the tendency to "weed out" deviant individuals, some of whom might nevertheless become effective, perhaps outstanding, leaders.

Even if there is no single universal pattern of characteristics of the leader, it is conceivable at least that there might be certain universal characteristics *of the relationship* between the leader and the other situational factors which are essential for optimum organized human effort in all situations. This is doubtful. Consider, for example, the relationship of an industrial manager with a group of native employees in an underdeveloped country on the one hand, and with a group of United States workmen who are members of a well-established international union on the other. Moreover, even if research finally indicates that there are such universal requirements of the relationship, there will still be more than one way of achieving them. For example, if "mutual confidence" between the leader and the led is a universal requirement, it is obvious that there are many ways of developing and maintaining this confidence.

We have already considered some of the significant conditions for the success of certain relationships involving interdependence in industrial organizations today. To achieve these conditions, the supervisor requires skills and attitudes, *but these can be acquired by people who differ widely in their inborn traits and abilities.* In fact, one of the important lessons from research and experience in this field is that the attempt to train supervisors to adopt a single leadership "style" yields poorer results than encouraging them to create the essential conditions *in their individual ways* and with due regard for their own particular situations. Note also in this connection how organization structure and management philosophy may either encourage or inhibit the supervisor in establishing these conditions.

It does not follow from these considerations that *any* individual can become a successful leader in a given situation. It *does* follow that successful leadership is not dependent on the possession of a single universal pattern of inborn traits and abilities. It seems likely that leadership potential (considering the tremendous variety of situations for which leadership is required) is broadly rather than narrowly distributed in the population.

Research findings to date suggest, then, that it is more fruitful to consider leadership as a relationship between the leader and the situation than as a universal pattern of characteristics possessed by certain people. The differences in requirements for successful leadership in different situations are more striking than the similarities. Moreover, research studies emphasize the importance of leadership skills and attitudes which can be acquired and are, therefore, not inborn characteristics of the individual.

It has often happened in the physical sciences that what was once believed to be an inherent property of objects—gravity, for example, or electrical "magnetism," or mass—has turned out to be a complex relationship between internal and external factors. The same thing happens in the social sciences, and leadership is but one example.

Implications for Management

What is the practical relevance for management of these findings of social science research in the field of leadership? First, if we accept the point of view that leadership consists of a relationship between the leader, his followers, the organization, and the social milieu, and if we recognize that these situational factors are subject to substantial changes with time, we must recognize that we cannot predict the personal characteristics of the managerial resources that an organization will require a decade or two hence. Even if we can list the positions to be filled, we cannot define very adequately the essential characteristics of the people who will be needed in those situations at that time. *One of management's major tasks, therefore, is to provide a heterogeneous supply of human resources from which individuals can be selected to fill a variety of specific but unpredictable needs.*

This is a blow to those who have hoped that the outcome of research would be to provide them with methods by which they could select today the top management of tomorrow. It is a boon to those who have feared the consequences of the "crown prince" approach to management development. It carries other practical implications of some importance.

With the modern emphasis on career employment and promotion from within, management must pay more than casual attention to its recruitment practices. It would seem logical that this process should tap a variety of sources: liberal arts as well as technical graduates, small colleges as well as big universities, institutions in different geographic regions, etc. It may be necessary, moreover, to look carefully at the criteria for selection of college recruits if heterogeneity is a goal. The college senior who graduates in the top 10 per cent of his class may come from a narrow segment of the range of potential leaders for industry. What of the student who has, perhaps for reasons unrelated to intellectual capacity, graduated in the middle of his class because he got A's in some subjects and C's and D's in others? What of the student whose academic achievement was only average because the education system never really challenged him?

As a matter of fact there is not much evidence that high academic achievement represents a necessary characteristic for industrial leadership. There may be a positive correlation, but it is not large enough to provide a basis for a recruitment policy. In fact, the current President of the United States would have been passed over at graduation by any management recruiter who relied on this correlation! It may be, on the contrary, that the *intellectual* capacity required for effective leadership in many industrial management positions is no greater than that required for graduation from a good college. Of course, there are positions requiring high intellectual capacity, but it does not follow that there is a one-to-one correlation between this characteristic and success as an industrial leader. (This question of intellectual capacity is, of course, only one reason why industry seeks the bulk of its potential managerial resources among college graduates today. There are other factors involved: confidence and social poise, skill acquired through participation in extracurricular activities, personal ambition and drive, etc. These, however, are relatively independent of class standing.)

It may be argued that intellectual *achievement,* as measured by consistently high grades in all subjects, is evidence of motivation and willingness to work. Perhaps it is—in the academic setting—but it is also evidence of willingness to conform to the quite arbitrary demands of the educational system. There is little reason for assuming that high motivation and hard work *in school* are the best predictors of motivation and effort in later life. There are a good many examples to the contrary.

A second implication from research findings about leadership is that a management development program should involve many people within the organization rather than a select few. The fact that some companies have been reasonably successful in developing a selected small group of managerial trainees may well be an artifact—an example of the operation of the "self-fulfilling prophecy." If these companies had been equally concerned to develop managerial talent within a much broader sample, they might have accomplished this purpose with no greater percentage of failures. And, if the generalizations above are sound, they would have had a richer, more valuable pool of leadership resources to draw on as a result.

Third, management should have as a goal the development of the unique capacities and potentialities of each individual rather than common objectives for all participants. This is a purpose which is honored on paper much more than in practice. It is difficult to achieve, particularly in the big company, but if we want heterogeneous leadership resources to meet the unpredictable needs of the future we certainly won't get them by subjecting all our managerial trainees to the same treatment.

Moreover, this process of developing heterogeneous resources must be continuous; it is never completed. Few human beings ever realize all of their potentialities for growth, even though some may reach a practical limit with respect to certain capacities. Each individual is unique, and it is this uniqueness we will constantly encourage and nourish if we are truly concerned to develop leaders for the industry of tomorrow.

Fourth, the promotion policies of the company should be so administered that these heterogeneous resources are actually considered when openings occur. There is little value in developing a wide range of talent if only a small and possibly limited segment of it constitutes the field of candidates when a particular position is being filled.

In view of the selective operation of situational variables referred to above, there may be legitimate questions concerning the value of an *exclusive* policy of "promotion from within." It is conceivable that in a large and reasonably decentralized company sufficient heterogeneity can be maintained by transfers of managerial talent between divisions, but it is probable that fairly strenuous efforts will be required to offset the normal tendency to create and maintain a "type," a homogeneous pattern of leadership within a given organization. Without such efforts competent individuals who don't "fit the pattern" are likely to be passed over or to leave because their talents are not rewarded. Many industrial organizations, for example, would not easily tolerate the strong individualism of a young Charles Kettering today.

Finally, if leadership is a function—a complex relation between leader and situation—we ought to be clear that every promising recruit is *not* a potential member of top management. Some people in some companies will become outstanding leaders as foremen, or as plant superintendents, or as professional specialists. Many of these would not be effective leaders in top management positions, at least under the circumstances prevailing in the company.

If we take seriously the implications of the research findings in this field, we will place high value on such people. We will seek to enable them to develop to the fullest their potentialities in the role they can fill best. And we will find ways to reward them which will persuade them that we consider outstanding leadership *at any level* to be a precious thing.

REFERENCES

Bennis, Warren G., "Leadership Theory and Administrative Behavior," *Administrative Science Quarterly*, vol. 4, no. 3, 1959.

Fortune Editors, *The Executive Life*. New York: Doubleday & Company, Inc., 1956.

Gibb, Cecil A., "Leadership," in Gardner Lindzey (ed.), *Handbook of Social Psychology*. Reading, Mass.: Addison-Wesley Publishing Company, 1954, vol. II.

Ginzberg, Eli, *What Makes an Executive*. New York: Columbia University Press, 1955.

Knickerbocker, Irving, "Leadership: A Conception and Some Implications," *Journal of Social Issues*, vol. 4, no. 3, 1948.

Selznick, Philip, *Leadership in Administration*. Evanston, Ill.: Row, Peterson & Company, 1957.

14

Management Development Programs

There was a time when it was widely believed that management development was an automatic process requiring little attention. It was felt that the normal operation of the industrial organization would permit the cream to rise to the top, where it would become visible and could be skimmed off as needed. It will become apparent as we examine the subject that there is more than a little to be said in favor of this theory *provided conditions are created which permit the cream to rise.* However, most managements of large companies have discarded this theory and proceeded along other lines. Particularly since World War II we have seen an unprecedented growth in management development programs and activities throughout the whole Western World. It is rare to find a large or even medium-sized company today which does not have a formal program and a staff to administer it.

If we grant that management development cannot be left entirely to chance, there are several alternatives open. Many companies have followed one of these which might be characterized as the "manufacturing" approach. Management has not phrased its philosophy this way, but it has looked on the problem essentially as a production problem. People have been assigned the *engineering* task of *designing* a program and *building* the necessary *machinery,* toward the end of *producing* the needed *supply* of managerial talent. The evidence of this philosophy is to be seen on every hand. We have management inventories, replacement charts with elaborate codes and colors, formal machinery for recruiting and selecting potential managerial talent, special indoctrination programs for the new recruits, appraisal programs, job rotation, and a welter of training activities. The production of managerial talent is itself a big business.

This manufacturing philosophy of management development is a natural concomitant of management by direction and control. The requirements of the organization are paramount. Individuals are selected, oriented, appraised, rotated, promoted, sent to school —all within an administrative framework which leaves them relatively little voice in their own career development. The concept of integration is not so much ignored as assumed to be automatic: Of course, people "with potential" want to get ahead, acquire status, obtain economic rewards, be developed. They should welcome, therefore, these many activities and programs which provide for their needs.

Most people do want the things that management development programs provide. However, each individual is unique in terms of his capacities, his interests and goals, his talents. The manufacturing approach to management development does many things *to* him and *for* him, but generally with the tacit assumption that what is good for the organization is good for him. The specific, uniquely individual, mutually adaptive characteristics of the integrative process tend to be missed by this approach.

In the last analysis the individual must develop himself, and he will do so optimally only in terms of what *he* sees as meaningful and valuable. If he becomes an active party to the decisions that are made about his development, he is likely to make the most of the opportunities that are presented. If, on the other hand, he is simply a passive agent being rotated or sent to school, or promoted, or otherwise manipulated, he is less likely to be motivated to develop himself.

It would be a mistake to dismiss the accomplishments in this field as insignificant. Management's concern with the problem has been real, and its efforts have by no means been unsuccessful. One cannot escape the impression, however, that the individual frequently "gets lost in the machinery," and that this is not merely a consequence of company size or of the complexity of the problem. It is to a considerably greater extent a consequence of management's conception that the task is one of manufacturing talent from available raw materials.

An alternative approach to management development is somewhat analogous to that of agriculture. It is concerned with "growing" talent rather than manufacturing it. The fundamental idea behind such an approach is that the individual will grow into what he is capable of becoming, provided we can create the proper conditions for that growth. Such an approach involves less emphasis on manufacturing techniques and more on controlling the climate and the fertility of the soil, and on methods of cultivation.

Taking this point of view, let us consider some of the important environmental conditions which affect the growth of managers. We will look at three groups of factors: (1) economic and technological characteristics of the industry and the firm, (2) policies and practices of the company, and (3) the behavior of the immediate superior.

Economic and Technological Characteristics of the Firm

Obviously, a rapidly growing industry, characterized by substantial and continuous technological innovation, represents a different environment for managerial growth than a static or contracting industry facing severe economic difficulties, and in which there is little technological innovation. There may be differences of opinion concerning the degree to which top management can control these broad environmental characteristics, but there is no question that they do influence the nature and the rate of managerial development.

The difference was brought home sharply to me recently when I spent a couple of days in each of two companies. The first was a division of a large company which was developing one of the new intercontinental ballistic missiles. The people who make up this organization are young; they are tremendously excited over the challenge represented by their task. The technology of the industry is growing so fast that it is almost impossible to keep up with it. Changes and innovations—some of them revolutionary—take place almost daily. Growth is rapid, and opportunities for advancement and new experience occur faster than people can quite meet them. Almost no one seemed to feel that he was genuinely "on top of his job," and yet it was clear that the organization was doing an effective job, that morale was high, and that people were growing.

I went directly from this company to the headquarters of a major railroad. The contrast in atmosphere left me bemused for days. The managers with whom I talked there showed almost none of the excitement and challenge which had been so vividly demonstrated in the other organization. They expressed generally cynical views about the opportunities for growth and development; they talked about the rigidities of the organization and about the lack of challenge in their work. While there was a fundamental enthusiasm among them for railroading, I got the impression that it was focused on the romantic past rather than on the future. Promotions and new job opportunities were seen as depending primarily upon openings created by death or retirement. The climate for managerial growth under these conditions is certainly not optimum, even though this particular company is one that is making sincere and reasonably effective efforts to overcome its economic difficulties and to improve the caliber of its management generally.

These aspects of the organizational environment are perhaps relatively uncontrollable, at least in short-run terms. They are like the differences between the conditions faced by the vegetable grower in the San Joaquin Valley of California and the New Hampshire farmer. Nevertheless, within a given environment, the nature and the quality of the processes of growth can be influenced by managerial philosophy and practice. Successful crops *are* grown in New Hampshire.

The Effects of Company Structure, Policy, and Practice

Growth and development of the human being—changes in attitudes, perceptions, and behavior—are processes which involve learning. Learning, in turn, is a function of rewards and punishments. These may be external and tangible (a salary increase, praise from the boss, increased status, etc.) or internal and intangible (the satisfaction of solving a tough problem, of acquiring new knowledge or new skill, or the frustration of being blocked in pursuing one's goals). The development of the individual is materially influenced by the kinds of rewards and satisfactions on the one hand, or punishments and frustrations on the other, which are characteristic of his company. Organization structure and management philosophy as represented in policies and their associated practices involve a variety of rewards and punishments and thus affect his growth.

For example, a centralized organization structure, with rigid lines between departments and functions and many hierarchical levels, restricts the opportunities for the individual manager to assume responsibility, to try out new ideas, to exercise judgment. Such a structure limits growth. This is one of the major arguments for decentralization and for a wide span of control such as is inherent in flat organizations. A decentralized organization provides an environment in which the individual, through taking greater responsibility for his own behavior, obtains intrinsic rewards in the form of ego and self-actualization satisfactions, which in turn encourage him to take still more responsibility and thus to grow.

The control over behavior exerted by managerial procedures also affects growth. As we have already seen, tight systems of control negate the positive advantages of decentralization. If his superiors keep him under constant surveillance by means of detailed reports on his behavior, he has no real freedom of action.

Is the company operated in such a way that the individual manager is rewarded for narrow departmental loyalties and for efforts devoted exclusively to improving the operation of his particular function, or is he rewarded for behavior which contributes to the objectives of the organization as a whole? Obviously, top management wants its subordinates to be concerned with the business as a whole; but the actual rewards and punishments (from the type of structure, from performance criteria, from policies and control systems, and from the behavior and attitudes of his boss and his peers) may well have the opposite effect. Learning will occur, but not growth in the desired direction.

What are the rewards for the individual who elects to pursue a staff career, or for the brilliant researcher who is not motivated to enter research administration? Is the salary structure one which offers comparable rewards for staff and line at any given level? Does it, for example, put a ceiling on the salary of the researcher unless he becomes a manager? And, beyond salary, what are the prevailing attitudes in the company toward jobs other than those in line management? Are they considered to be a "burden," second-class forms of "busywork"? The organization needs people who will grow in the direction of specialized professional competence as well as those who will become high-level line managers. Do the rewards and punishments—both formal and informal—encourage both these forms of growth?

What about the way in which promotions are administered? Is promotion considered to be the only real measure of success for the individual? In some companies, the environment of attitude and practice is such that the individual who is not promotable is considered to be a failure. It is said of him that he "lacks potential," or that he "has reached his ceiling." Not only is this attitude in itself punishing, but the rewards for further growth—salary, status, recognition, etc.—are lacking (the formal machinery cannot encompass such exceptions). This, despite the probability that he could, if adequate rewards were available, continue to grow and to increase his contribution to the organization at his present level. Can the individual who for personal reasons does not want to climb higher on the organizational ladder, but instead wishes to make his contribution to the enterprise an outstanding one at his present level, remain there without being punished in a variety of subtle ways for having made this choice?

In an organization where promotion is the sole measure of success, most people are oriented to the job to which they hope to move next. Naturally, they want to be promoted in order to prove their value, so their performance on the present job is geared exclusively to those things which will get them out of it! This, too, is learning resulting from rewards and punishments, but is it growth in the direction management desires?

Is there what Larry Appley has so appropriately termed "the timely elimination of the incompetent"? This form of punishment has substantial effects not only on those who may be asked to leave the organization, but on others who remain. It indicates something about management's standards of performance, about what kind of behavior will be rewarded.

Universities are often criticized by industrial management for their permanent tenure system under which a faculty member achieves job security under certain conditions and after a probationary period of several years' duration. They see this as encouraging mediocre performance because the individual with tenure is not subject to the threat of being fired, except under rare and extreme conditions. However, most industrial organizations have an informal tenure system which is equivalent in its operation to the formal policies of the university. It is relatively rare after eight or ten years for an individual to be fired for incompetence; after fifteen or twenty years it is almost unheard of. The difficulty is that in industry the individual slips into the status of permanent tenure without a definite decision as to whether he merits it. He acquires tenure by default.

The advantage of the university tenure system is that it provides a formal decision point. At a stated time, a careful evaluation is made of the individual and of the probability of his long-run contribution to the institution. Up to this time, any reasonable benefit of doubt with respect to his performance is resolved in favor of the individual; he is given another chance. At this point, however, the benefit of doubt shifts and is resolved in favor of the institution. If there are doubts concerning his long-term contribution, the refusal of permanent tenure results, and the individual leaves. Properly administered, this formal tenure policy can lead to the timely elimination of the incompetent. Far from being a handicap, it is a genuine asset which has considerable impact on the growth of all members of the university faculty.

Another policy which, with its associated practices, materially affects growth is that of job rotation to give the individual a wider range of experience and to test out his abilities. Companies differ greatly in the way they apply this principle, and the differences in administration yield quite different rewards and punishments.

In one company managers are moved so rapidly from job to job throughout a large geographic area that the common label for rotation among them is "suitcase supervision." The consequence of this kind of rotation is not the growth that management desires. The individual moves into a job knowing that he is likely to be there for a very short time. He does not take full responsibility; his concern is simply to keep things on an even keel until he is relieved. He does not innovate, he does not take risks, he does not, in fact, operate as a manager, but as though he were an assistant "acting" during the temporary absence of the boss.

There is some question as to whether the learning that takes place under such conditions is really as great as it would be if the individual merely *observed* the regular manager in action for an equivalent period. Keeping the chair warm is not conducive to growth.

Toward the other extreme are companies who utilize the rotational principle only in a very limited sense. Rotation is confined to moves within a given department or function, at least until the individual has climbed a good way up the ladder. When he does get an opportunity to move into a different function he may be past forty and in a rather substantial job. Unless he is to be demoted, a move will put him in a key spot in another department or function. This is often risky. The pressures on him will be severe. But what is more important is that he is unlikely to give the leadership and the guidance in the new job that the organization under him requires. He has to be carried along by his subordinates. If by any chance he is unwilling to accept this form of help and attempts an autocratic kind of leadership, he is likely to make serious mistakes. Meanwhile, the organization under him suffers, particularly if the rotation into this spot is frequent.

A critical factor affecting the growth of the individual on a rotational job is the behavior of the superior to whom he now reports

The new boss can make the rotation a genuine learning experience for the incumbent, but only if he devotes considerable time and thought to doing so. This he is unlikely to do unless *his* superiors in turn recognize his efforts and reward him for it. We will consider a little later what this means. At the moment, it is enough to ask whether those who administer programs of job rotation take this important growth factor into account.

Rotation serves to minimize the dangers of personal prejudice in assessments of the individual's performance and potential. We noted earlier in examining appraisal methods that such judgments may be as much a function of the superior's attitude and methods of managing as of the subordinate's behavior. However, if the individual spends a reasonable amount of time under a succession of managers, the effects of these factors are likely to be reduced.

Clearly, job rotation can be an effective means of affording opportunities for the growth of managers. Whether it is will depend on when the individual is moved, into what positions, for how long, under what kind of supervision, and upon the degree to which his own career goals are taken into account. All of these aspects of the administration of rotational programs involve important rewards and punishments. To conceive of rotation *in itself* as significant, leaving these related factors to chance, is to utilize a machinery in a way which is likely to hamper rather than to facilitate growth.

The Behavior of the Immediate Superior

Within the broader context of the climate created by company policy and practice, organization structure, and general philosophy, there is the climate created by the individual manager's immediate superior. As we saw in Chapter 10, the climate of this relationship is critical. It is probably the most important influence affecting managerial development.

Every encounter between a superior and subordinate involves

learning of some kind for the subordinate. (It should involve learning for the superior, too, but that is another matter.) When the boss gives an order, asks for a job to be done, reprimands, praises, conducts an appraisal interview, deals with a mistake, holds a staff meeting, works with his subordinates in solving a problem, gives a salary increase, discusses a possible promotion, or takes any other action with subordinates, he is teaching them something. The attitudes, the habits, the expectations of the subordinate will be either reinforced or modified to some degree as a result of every encounter with the boss. This is why "on-the-job training" is such a significant process. It is why the results of classroom supervisory training are often discouraging. The day-by-day experience on the job is so much more powerful that it tends to overshadow what the individual may learn in other settings.

Whether the manager is aware of his powerful influence for better or worse upon his subordinates' growth, and whether he considers this responsibility a significant one to which he will devote extensive thought, time, and energy, will depend on the environment in which *he* operates. It is typical to say that each manager is responsible for the growth and development of subordinates, but the reward and punishment system of the company is not always consistent with this statement. An example from the academic field may serve to make the point.

> Most universities stress as part of their promotion policy two major responsibilities of the faculty member: teaching and scholarly research. While it is recognized that individuals will not always be equally competent in both of these, the formal policy usually indicates that promotions will go to those who are outstanding in one and at least satisfactory in the other.
>
> This is policy; practice is usually something else. It is commonly believed, and there is at least some evidence for the belief, that promotions are in practice based primarily on

scholarship as indicated by quantity of publication and by colleague judgments of research competence. Promotions go with considerable frequency to faculty members who are competent and productive scholars, but who are poor and ineffective teachers. The reward and punishment system operates in such a way that there is little encouragement for the average faculty member in the big university to devote time and energy to improving his teaching skills. In fact, he may be defeating his own career goals if he emphasizes his teaching at the expense of his research and publication.

In industry, rewards in the form of promotions, salary increases, and recognition generally go to those who demonstrate competence in activities other than the development of their subordinates. In querying management representatives of a number of companies whose activities with respect to management development are extensive, I have discovered only a couple of cases in which it is felt that achievement in the development of subordinates is given genuine recognition. However, unless the manager is made truly accountable for creating a climate conducive to growth, and unless rewards and punishments for him are clearly related to his performance along these lines, we can expect that it will be given scant attention.

Some managers, aware of their dependence downward, do give a great deal of attention to the development of their subordinates, even though their efforts may not be recognized and rewarded "upstairs." They recognize that their own ability to manage depends to an important extent on the performance of those below them. Others, who do not recognize this downward dependence (and these are in the majority), are more concerned with their own performance and their own rewards and punishments than with the growth of their subordinates. In fact, they are fearful of having subordinates who are too competent—they worry about having their own weaknesses shown up. This self-protective orientation creates a climate which hampers rather than facilitates growth.

Perhaps it is now apparent why the "manufacturing" approach to management development is less effective than one might wish: It focuses management's attention on the wrong things. The formal programs may even have negative effects if the environment is not itself conducive to growth. The research findings that supervisory training courses are ineffective unless the things they teach are reinforced by the daily environment on the job is but one example. The same thing is true concerning the results obtained from every form of management development "machinery." If we want growth of managerial talent, we must give attention to the conditions which affect it. Some of these are subtle and difficult to influence, others are obvious and subject to modification once we pause to examine them.

The Role of the Management Development Staff

If there is a staff department concerned with management development along the lines suggested by Theory Y, it is obvious that one of its major activities will be a professional one: strategy planning with top management. Such a staff will be concerned with the organizational environment, broadly as well as narrowly. It will study company policies and practices and endeavor to help management to understand their significance for growth so that organization structure, company policy, and day-to-day managerial behavior will aid the development of managerial talent.

Such a staff will have as its second function that of providing competent counsel and help to managers who are attempting to fulfill their responsibilities for the development of their subordinates. This help cannot be forced on the organization or "sold" to it. A competent staff will, under proper conditions, find itself sought for this purpose. The help it will be prepared to give will seldom take the form of detailed formal procedures or canned training courses. It will be help to managers—individually or collectively—in finding and utilizing whatever means will best meet *their* needs. The analogy of the architect vis-à-vis his clients suggested in Chapter 12 is particularly relevant in this connection. As a third and distinctly minor aspect of the function, such a staff will be concerned with problems of administration. Certain data for purposes of replacement planning and management inventory will be required. However, a staff group concerned with problems of growth will not be trapped into reliance on mechanically coded color charts and statistical analyses as a substitute for concern with the conditions influencing growth. Records and statistics are not methods for developing managerial talent; they are means of keeping track of the process.

A staff group in a large company made a concentrated attempt several years ago to follow the "manufacturing" approach to management development by creating an elaborate formal program and attempting to sell it to management. After some time, this group became aware that the desired purposes were not being achieved. The program was not operating well; most managers were not using the procedures or the forms, and there was rather generally a passive resistance to the whole field of management development.

Instead of concluding (as some management development staff groups have under these familiar circumstances) that the remedy was more "selling," or a training program to teach management how to use the formal machinery, this group decided to start again using an entirely different approach. This involved just one activity: annual meetings of the president of the company with each of his immediate subordinates, individually, in which the subordinate reported in detail to the president on his activities and accomplishments in creating an environment conducive to the growth of his subordinates. Each individual reporting to him, and each individual at the second level below him, were discussed with the president in detail. The emphasis was on what the manager was doing to make it possible for his subordinates to further their own self-development. The president made it clear—not only in words, but also in action—that he held his own subordinates accountable for this managerial function, and that how well they fulfilled the responsibilities in these respects would make a substantial difference in their own rewards and punishments.

After a couple of years, the effects of this single activity were substantial. The management development staff were being asked for help by some of the same managers who, two or three years before, were resistant and antagonistic toward the whole function. The managers reporting to the president found that they could not fulfill this responsibility without encouraging a similar process among those reporting to them, and so the general emphasis upon accountability for management development began to move down in the organization. The managers themselves learned a good deal as they attempted to fulfill this new responsibility.

This approach involved little formal machinery. Each manager was encouraged to develop his own methods for presenting his analysis to the president and his own ways of working with his subordinates to further their growth. The management development staff were ready and willing to provide professional help to those who sought it.

The experience of this company adds one more bit of evidence to a generalization which my observation of the field of management development has tended to support: There is almost no relationship between the amount of formal programing and machinery of management development and the actual achievement of the organization in this respect. I sometimes think the correlation may be negative! Programs and procedures do not *cause* management development, because it is not possible to "produce" managers the way we produce products. We can only hope to "grow" them, and growth depends less on the tools we use than on the environment which is created. If it is conducive to growth, the main job may be keeping the soil in good tilth and keeping the weeds down.

There is probably no single activity which will do more to create an environment conducive to managerial growth than the "target-setting" approach described in Chapter 5. However, as we saw in considering this subject, what is involved is a theory of management, not a formula or a mechanical procedure. The concept of management by integration and self-control cannot be successfully developed as a packaged program and sold to management, but a competent professional staff can help management discover its value. In doing so they will not face the difficult task of persuading management to add to its already heavy load. On the contrary, they will be helping management to manage in a way which accomplishes organizational objectives better *and at the same time* encourages the growth of subordinates. If a climate and soil conditions conducive to growth are created by the way management manages, the cream *will* rise to the top, in the sense that individual managers throughout the whole organization will be involved in a process of self-development leading to the realization of their potentialities. In this way, effective management of the enterprise and the development of managerial talent become a single integrated activity, and managers no longer face a conflict between these two responsibilities.

REFERENCES

Acton Society Trust, *Management Succession.* London: 1956.
American Management Association, *Organization Planning and Management Development,* Personnel Series, no. 141, 1951.
Dooher, Joseph M., and Vivienne Marquis (eds.), *The Development of Executive Talent: A Handbook of Management Develop-*

ment Techniques and Case Studies. New York: American Management Association, 1952.

Mace, Myles L., *The Growth and Development of Executives.* Boston: Division of Research, Graduate School of Business Administration, Harvard University, 1950.

Martin, Norman H., and Anselm L. Strauss, "Patterns of Mobility within Industrial Organizations," *The Journal of Business,* vol. 29, no. 2, 1956.

National Industrial Conference Board, Inc., "Management Development: A Ten-year Case Study," Studies in Personnel Policy, no. 140, 1953.

15

Acquiring Managerial Skills
in the Classroom

The job environment of the individual is the most important variable affecting his development. Unless that environment is conducive to his growth, none of the other things we do to him or for him will be effective. This is why the "agricultural" approach to management development is preferable to the "manufacturing" approach. The latter leads, among other things, to the unrealistic expectation that we can create and develop managers in the classroom.

A colleague once said that the chief purpose of formal education for the manager is to increase his ability to learn from experience. To this I would add a second purpose: to increase his ability to help his subordinates learn from experience, i.e., to enable him to learn how to create an environment conducive to their growth.

In considering classroom learning for managers (in the plant or in the academic institution), it is necessary to make some distinctions. There are various kinds of learning, and the methods which are appropriate vary with the kind of learning which is sought.

Acquiring Intellectual Knowledge

An electrical engineer may need more knowledge than he now possesses about circuit design. A new employee may require knowledge about company policies and work rules. A plant manager may need an awareness of the potentialities of linear programing. A foreman may require information about the new provisions in the labor agreement.

The acquisition of knowledge is a fairly straightforward process *provided the individual wants the new knowledge.* It can be made available to him in several ways. However, if he doesn't want the knowledge or if he doesn't know he needs it, we will have considerable difficulty getting him to learn it. Many of the methods we utilize in this kind of education are designed to influence his motivation to learn. In school, the formal grade is a major device for this purpose, although the method of presentation of the material may also be important. In industry the attempts to create a "felt need" for the new knowledge are many: implied or promised rewards, such as more chance for promotion, making the job easier, pleasing the boss, keeping out of trouble, and implied or promised punishments which are mostly the obverse of such rewards.

The problems involved in this kind of managerial education arise primarily from neglect of the principle of integration. The individual may recognize his need for knowledge in some area, or his superior may show him how it would be valuable. If there are courses available in nearby academic institutions or in a company-operated program, he is likely to acquire the necessary knowledge with no more ado. Partial tuition refunds, or time off from work, may provide an incentive, but if the individual is persuaded of his need such rewards will make little difference.

It is the elaboration, and particularly the standardization, of this process for large numbers of people which lessens its value. It is all too easy for higher-level management or staff groups to decide for others what they need in the way of additional knowledge. Courses and programs are then prepared and offered. If these are genuine "offerings," and the individuals can really choose whether to accept them, few problems will arise except that some such programs will be less patronized than may have been expected.

What tends to happen is that upper management becomes convinced that a given program is a Good Thing for subordinates. (A British colleague refers to supervisory training as "the aspirin of higher management"!) The "offering" then becomes a scheduled assignment for whole categories of people (sometimes all of management, but more often lower levels only). The need for the new knowledge is now not the individual's "felt" need, but a need which others think he ought to have. The integrative principle is abandoned in favor of a form of control which can be used only where dependence is high (for example, in the elementary public school), and which is not very effective even then. "Giving" courses in this manner is generally not an appropriate method of influence. The learning is limited because the motivation is low. Moreover, this strategy soon generates negative attitudes toward training in general and thus hampers the creation of an organizational climate conducive to growth.

There may be courses which do, in fact, meet widespread "felt" needs, or which are so well presented that they arouse such needs. These are bound to be few, because individual situations vary so greatly even within a single category such as first-line supervision. Admittedly, it is difficult to create a climate such that individuals can exercise freedom of choice with respect to courses or programs which their superiors believe to be a Good Thing. Yet the failure to do so is one of the major reasons why much classroom education of managers is relatively ineffective. It is asking too much to expect the trainer to create the necessary motivation for learning under such circumstances, regardless of his skills or the methods he uses.

Even where the circumstances dictate the desirability of a course for a large group of managers, there can be some adjustment to the individual. Certainly not all first-line supervisors, for example, are equally ready at one time to benefit from any given course. Certainly some do not perceive that they need it at all (and are, therefore, likely to benefit but little from it). It is possible to create a climate within which such courses are taken on a truly voluntary basis. The word "truly" is important. The voluntary character is distinctly altered if people perceive that they are expected to "volunteer," and that they may face the disapproval of the boss if they don't.

If there are needs which can be met by a given kind of training, some at least of those "in need" are likely to be aware of it. An initial step can often be planned *with them*. If the resulting activity meets their needs, they will be the ones who create a demand among others for it. This is what happened, for example, in one plant a few years ago.

A few of the younger and more ambitious foremen came to the personnel director to discuss their concern that they were not increasing their managerial competence at a rate sufficient to meet the requirements of the situation. They felt that their future careers in the company would be adversely affected unless they acquired more skill as managers. The initial work done to try to help these men flowered eventually into a variety of training activities that were actively sought by most of the supervisory force.

It may be worth noting that the first of these activities was not a training course, but a series of meetings having as an objective a clearer understanding of the foremen's responsibilities. During the course of these discussions many beyond the original group became involved. The outcome was a statement concerning the foremen's responsibilities which was accepted almost without change by the top management of the company. There was considerable learning for all concerned in this activity, although no one—including the personnel director—thought of it as "training." The same thing was true of several other projects undertaken subsequently by these supervisors with the help of the personnel staff.

The acquisition of knowledge or information requires the motivation of the learner. He can, of course, be motivated by threats of punishment. The risks involved in this method of control (even when the threat is the unspoken implication that he will be regarded less highly by his superiors if he doesn't attend the course) are the usual countermeasures correlated with management by direction and control.

Above all, it is necessary to recognize that knowledge cannot be pumped into human beings the way grease is forced into a fitting on a machine. The individual may learn; he is not taught. Effective education is always a process of influence by integration and self-control.

Up to this point the emphasis has been on the acquisition of knowledge in the specific sense. What about the "broadening" of the manager through a more general educational experience which includes a wide range of intellectual fare? These experiences are usually provided through university programs of several months' duration. A few companies, partly because of their size, but more often because of their unique needs as they perceive them, have established academic facilities within the organization to provide this form of education.

It is an obvious and important fact that the managerial task is becoming increasingly complex today. The effective manager must be clearly aware of social, political, and economic trends in society. He needs a general intellectual knowledge of a number of specialized fields so that he can grasp the scope of his own responsibilities, understand the role of his company in the economy and in the political milieu, and know when he needs professional help.

This form of education for the manager is important not only as a stimulus to innovation but as a requirement for adjustment to a rapidly changing world. The education of the manager should be a continuing process, and it can be aided periodically by his participation in these formal academic programs. Moreover, after he has been out of school for a while and faced up to some of the realities of organizational life, he often is in a position to learn much more than would have been possible earlier. It is common experience among those of us who teach in these programs that experienced managers understand and grasp our subject matter more readily than college students who have not yet had much exposure to the industrial world.

The university is the proper place for education like this. University faculty members can provide a perspective which is difficult to acquire within the industrial organization. By and large, the best teaching talent for these purposes is to be found in the university setting and is unlikely to be attracted into full-time industrial positions. In the university setting it is acceptable to be critical of the *status quo;* there are few sacred cows that must be respected. Ideas can be followed where they lead, rather than being tempered by sensitivity to the prejudices of a boss. Finally, it is the function of the university to provide leadership in intellectual fields, and it is, therefore, to the academic world that industry should look for the best, the most up-to-date, and the most critical thinking on the broad matters which affect the managerial task.

There is another important value for the industrial manager in the university program: the opportunity, through the exchange of experience and ideas with other managers, to discover something about the similarities as well as the differences between industries and companies. Many participants in these programs see this as the primary value of the whole experience. It is important to recognize, however, that this interchange occurs within the context of problems and theoretical issues that are raised by the university faculty. An ordinary bull session of the same group of managers outside of the university context would usually have less value because it would lack this structure.

Finally, it is important to recognize that activities other than the classroom lecture form a significant part of many of these university programs. For one thing, the requirement that the manager must do a considerable amount of reading of a kind to which he has probably been unaccustomed since his college days is of some importance. Many participants in these programs report that the experience has rekindled their interest in intellectual ideas, and that after their return home they have done more of this kind of reading than they had for a number of years previously. Then there are activities like, for example, the trip that the Sloan Fellows make to Washington during the course of their year at MIT. While there they have opportunities for discussion with key members of the executive, legislative, and judicial departments of our government. As a result they gain a perspective and an insight into industry-government relationships which would be difficult to achieve through classroom experience alone. In another of the MIT executive programs the group has several opportunities to meet with top research faculty in some of the major technical and scientific fields to explore with them the frontiers of knowledge and research, and to see through their eyes some of the most probable future developments which may affect management. This, too, is outside the formal classroom setting and is an experience which is difficult to arrange except on the university campus.

Many companies have spent a substantial amount of money in sending managers to university programs, and they have recently begun to ask pointed questions about the worth of such experiences. The "evaluation" of the impact of such education on the manager has been a subject of considerable concern in the last few years. There is a real danger that the pressure for evaluation may lead us to try to measure the wrong things and, therefore, to miss entirely the true value of experiences of this kind. The purpose of most of these generalized university courses is not, and should not be, direct practical application of the learning to the job. Their purpose is not to provide answers to problems, formulas, or tricks of the trade. It is to broaden the manager's understanding of his job, to challenge some of his preconceptions, to make him better able to learn from experience when he gets back home because he will have acquired a more realistic understanding of the causes and effects with which he must deal. To the extent that this kind of education is successful, it will not reveal itself in immediate or obvious changes in his behavior back home. The learning which takes place will more probably be reflected in fairly subtle ways of which he himself may often be unaware. Nevertheless, these changes in perception do affect behavior, sometimes profoundly. It is certainly reasonable that management should want to evaluate the achievements of university programs in management development, but it is important that we understand the purposes of these programs so that we evaluate the right things.

We come now to some questions of who should go to such programs and when. In this connection we can profitably concern ourselves with the matter of integration between the individual manager's needs, readiness for learning, and past experience on the one hand and organizational requirements on the other. We do not need to approach the problem on a mass basis or treat the individual as a pawn on a chessboard.

It is often ironic that management's purpose in sending a man to one of these programs is entirely different than the man's perception. It is not uncommon for managers to worry all through such programs about why they have been *sent*. What have they done wrong? Where have they failed? What weaknesses were they supposed to correct? Many participants in university programs ask themselves questions like these because their assignment to the programs has been handled poorly. When a manager is "sent" to school because his boss has decided he needs it, there is a threatening character to the assignment and there is likely to be less learning as a result.

Another fairly common practice in some companies is to send some men to university programs as a reward for faithful service, and not with the expectation that it will make any substantial difference in their subsequent behavior. This may be nice for the men, although it is likely to raise some anxieties. The important point, however, is the effect of scattering a number of such people in a group of managers who are strongly motivated to learn and who regard the opportunity as a challenge rather than a reward. Management would be well advised to consider carefully whether this practice of using university programs as rewards for conscientious service, or as a device to avoid the appearance of discrimination, is really a wise one.

In the context of joint target setting, the needs of the individual manager for further education are quite likely to appear. Moreover, he will often be the one to perceive his needs and to raise questions about how they might be met. These needs will not alone be for the correction of weaknesses, but for purposes of self-realization and the utilization of strengths. If, in this setting, the decision is reached that a university program would be helpful, the question of his anxieties and his motivation are likely to be resolved in directions which will benefit both him and the organization.

Acquiring Manual Skills

The manager does not require many ordinary manual skills in the performance of his job. Examples of such skills in other contexts are learning to drive a car, operate a lathe, play golf, play a musical instrument, type. The science student acquires certain skills in applying scientific method through his laboratory courses.

A brief glance at learning of this kind will be helpful later when we examine the learning of the skills of social interaction, which are of great importance to the manager. The two kinds of learning have many things in common, although manual skills are by far the more easily acquired.

The acquisition of a manual skill requires practice, or experience accompanied by feedback. Pure trial-and-error learning can be appreciably speeded up by guidance, but the individual cannot learn unless he performs and unless he receives cues which tell him about the success of his efforts. In most motor learning the cues are fairly direct and immediate; for example, the golf ball slices into the woods, or "ht" instead of "th" appears on the sheet of paper in the typewriter. The smooth, effortless performance of the expert represents, of course, a level of learning in which the cues are responded to without conscious awareness, and in which many originally discrete acts have blended into wholes.

It is more obvious in acquiring motor skills than in acquiring intellectual knowledge—but no more true—that learning is an active process rather than a passive one. The necessary effort will be expended only if there is a "felt" need on the part of the learner.

Acquiring Problem-solving Skills

Much of a manager's work is solving problems. These include organizing his own and his subordinates' activities, planning (for either anticipated or unanticipated circumstances), choosing his own managerial strategies, and a wide range of other decision-making activities. There are skills involved in diagnosing problems, acquiring and interpreting relevant data, assessing and testing alternative solutions, and getting feedback concerning the effectiveness of both the solution and the process used in arriving at it. These skills can be improved, and classroom education is one method utilized for this purpose.

As with any skill, practice (experience) and feedback are essential for learning. The most widely used classroom method for improving problem-solving skills is the case method. In the hands of a skillful teacher, it can be highly effective. There is some scattered evidence that—when used alone—diagnostic skills may be improved without materially affecting the quality of solutions. Perhaps this is because traditionally there has been relatively little emphasis on theory in the exclusive use of the case method. It is recognized that there is seldom a single "best answer" to complex problems such as are represented by the cases. However, if underlying theoretical assumptions are not consciously and critically examined, they are likely to determine the answer unwittingly despite the care given to the analysis of the problem.

When the manager is on the job, practice in problem solving is, of course, inevitable. However, an important source of feedback for improving skills is frequently overlooked. This is the critical examination of mistakes that have occurred in order to understand what happened and why. If such "post mortems" comprise no more than a search for the culprit in order to place the blame, they will provide learning of one kind. If, on the other hand, it is recognized that mistakes are an inevitable occurrence in the trial-and-error process of acquiring problem-solving skills, they can be the source of other and more valuable learning.

One unpublished study in a large company carried a strong implication that the way in which a manager dealt with his subordinates' mistakes was the most important factor in determining whether his delegation to them was effective, i.e., whether they learned to take responsibility for their own performance.

It is obvious that the analysis of successful problem-solving efforts can also provide effective feedback for learning.

This kind of education can be carried into the classroom through the use of role playing. The behavior of the participants in the problem-solving exercise is directly observed and becomes the object of critical examination afterward. While it is true that role playing is not real life, it is surprising how real it becomes under proper circumstances. Moreover, it is conducive to learning because it is a "safe" situation (the only consequences occur in the classroom) in which the individual can practice forms of behavior which he might not be willing to use in real life. In addition, the situation can be replayed to test alternative approaches, thus providing opportunities for feedback which are seldom available on the job.

Another method which yields increased insight and understanding, if not directly improved skill in problem solving, is exposure under certain conditions to the thinking of others who face similar problems to one's own. As already noted, managers from different companies and different industries who are thrown together for several weeks in university programs learn a lot from discussions with each other outside the classroom. The subjects discussed in class stimulate outside arguments and exchanges of experience from which any but the individual who already knows all the answers can learn.

In one such program these experiences are augmented still further by exposing the group of middle management students to a series of top-level executives from different companies. At each such off-the-record meeting, the guest is quizzed by the group about his most serious managerial problems and his way of dealing with them. It is interesting to observe the increase in critical sophistication of the students (reflecting increased insight and understanding) as the series proceeds.

Another method which has proved effective for learning of this kind is a "clinic" in which a closely related group of managers (a department head and his subordinates, for example) meet with a "trainer" to consider together the actual problems they are currently trying to solve on the job. This affords an opportunity for the trainer to help them look critically not only at the problems but at the methods they are using to solve them, and thus to acquire understanding of their "processes" of problem solving and to increase their skills with respect to them.

Typically, this method reveals an important aspect of managerial problem-solving activities beyond the purely intellectual: the interactions among people which are often crucial in determining success or failure. Some managerial problem solving is carried out individually, but ordinarily it occurs in a group of at least two people. In groups a complex set of factors come into play which reveal the need for skills of social interaction.

Acquiring Skills of Social Interaction

Recognition of the crucial importance of these skills for effective managerial problem solving has led to a welter of educational efforts: courses in communications, supervisory methods, leadership, counseling, brainstorming, group dynamics, the use of staff, etc. The relatively small amount of research evidence available indicates two things: (1) effective learning in this field requires the solution of some exceedingly complex problems, and (2) lasting changes in behavior as a result of conventional classroom methods are quite unlikely. The reasons are not far to seek.

Every adult human being has an elaborate history of past experience in this field, and additional learning is profoundly influenced by that history. From infancy on, his ability to achieve his goals and satisfy his needs—his "social survival"—has been a function of his skills in influencing others. Deep emotional currents —unconscious needs such as those related to dependency and counterdependency—are involved. He has a large "ego investment" in his knowledge and skill in this area, and the defenses he has built to protect that investment are strong and psychologically complex.

It may be said of most of us that in organizational situations involving our superiors or subordinates we *react* (unconsciously, of course) to internal needs and fears and hopes to a greater extent than we *act* with respect to the situation itself. We attempt to exercise power or to gain acceptance, to lead or to take a minor role, to fight or to withdraw, to demonstrate our talents or hide our foibles—not so much because the situation requires it as because our own internal adjustment does.

Learning new skills of social interaction in the context of these factors is a difficult matter indeed. Inspirational lectures, or discussion of the principles of supervision, or conferences on human relations can provide us with new words, perhaps new insights into the behavior of others, but seldom more than new rationalizations with which to defend our own present behavior. The intensity of our own ego investment in what we now know and do is great enough to warp our perceptions to fit our needs.

But what is even more important, we normally get little feedback of real value concerning the impact of our behavior on others. If they don't behave as we desire, it is easy to blame *their* stupidity, *their* adjustment, *their* peculiarities. Only under rather extreme conditions do our subordinates even attempt to tell us how our behavior affects them. When our superiors sometimes make the attempt, we find it difficult to understand what they are driving at, and mostly we disagree with their perceptions of us. Above all, it isn't considered good taste to give this kind of feedback in most social settings. Instead, it is discussed by our colleagues when we are not present to learn from it.

Finally, with the ego investment we all have in our present skills of social interaction, and with the defenses we have erected to protect our belief in their adequacy, we are seldom strongly motivated to change. Unconsciously, we fear inevitable failure if we "try on" ways of behaving that differ materially from those we have learned with such difficulty over so long a period. A new gimmick or minor technique certainly, but not a major shift in strategy involving the acquisition of new and strange skills.

None of the educational methods discussed above brings about real changes in the skills of social interaction. An occasional individual may have encountered failure and difficulty so often that he is prepared to learn new skills. Individuals whose skills are already similar to those being taught may improve them somewhat. But these are not the results that are hoped for.

There are two educational methods in current use which appear to bring about significant improvements in the skills of social interaction. Only modest claims can be made for either of them, but they are becoming more effective as knowledge accumulates. The first of these is psychotherapy. Unfortunately, this form of education has only limited usefulness for management development today. It is widely perceived as relevant only when individuals are in serious trouble. It lends itself only to individual, or at best small group, applications. Finally, it is very time-consuming.

Nevertheless, as social standards change so that mental illness is no longer seen as the only reason for psychotherapy, this form of education is becoming more widely used. Groups of social scientists, like those at the Menninger Clinic, are pioneering applications of psychotherapy to managerial problems. Individual managers who find themselves in need of help are persuaded with less difficulty than in the past to seek it through psychological counseling and therapy. It is likely that we will see major developments in this field during the next decade or two.

The other method is a form of "laboratory" training developed during the last dozen years by a number of social scientists affiliated with the National Training Laboratory for Group Development in Washington. This organization, a division of the National Education Association, carries on its activities through a series of annual programs in various parts of the country. The programs are staffed by social scientists, some of whom are faculty members in academic institutions; some are professionals engaged in private practice; and some are employees of industrial, social service, and government organizations. All these individuals have participated actively with NTL in the development of its methods or in research in the field.

The core of this educational method for improving the skills of social interaction is called the "T" (for training) Group. It consists of ten to fifteen individuals and a trainer who meet for a number of successive periods. A rather common pattern involves a two-week program during which the T Group meets daily for two hours. The T Group supplies its own content for learning in the form of the behavior of its members during its meetings. This behavior includes social interactions of all kinds which are utilized by the individuals to increase their understanding (1) of the impact of their own behavior on others, (2) of their reactions to the behavior of others, (3) of the phenomena of group activity and their significance. Since participation in the T Group involves practice and feedback of a unique nature, the opportunity is present for improving the skills of social interaction.

The feedback in a T Group is of special importance because it differs sharply from that which occurs normally in group situations. Some of it comes from the trainer, but most of it is provided by the members to each other. The "ground rules" which the group establishes for feedback are important. With the help of the trainer, the group usually comes to see the differences between providing help and attempting to control or punish a member, between analyzing and interpreting a member's adjustment (which is taboo) and informing him of the impact it has on others. It is frequently amazing to observe the high degree of sensitivity and skill which develops in such groups as the members help each other to learn.

Naturally, the T Group is designed to facilitate kinds of behavior which can be most useful for learning about social interaction. Typically, certain features of everyday group activity are blurred or removed. The trainer, for example, does not provide the leadership which a group of "students" would normally expect. This produces a kind of "power vacuum" and a great deal of behavior which, in time, becomes the basis for learning. There is no agenda, except as the group provides it. There are no norms of group operation (such as *Robert's Rules of Order*) except as the group decides to adopt them.

The T Group is for some time a confusing, tension-laden, frustrating experience for most participants. But these conditions have been found to be conducive to learning in this field. Naturally, some individuals learn a great deal, while others resist the whole process. It is rare, however, for an individual to end a two-week experience in a T Group feeling that he has learned nothing.

Surrounding the T Group in programs of this kind are theoretical lectures, "skill-practice" sessions, demonstrations, sessions devoted to providing individuals with consultation in analyzing their "back-home" problems, and sessions designed to improve the skills required in helping others. All of these activities are designed in advance by the staff to provide a patterned whole, rather than a scrap basket of unrelated experiences. Each program is different in some ways from past ones as staff learning and research findings accumulate and as innovations are conceived.

Finally, such programs are conducted in locations which are psychologically if not geographically remote from everyday life. Bethel, Maine, Columbia's Arden House, and such locations make it possible to create a "cultural island" in which the significance of the whole experience is intensified. This, too, appears to aid learning, partly because the unreality creates an environment in which individuals are more flexible in trying on new behaviors to see how they fit.

One of the very real problems connected with this highly unconventional approach to education in the skills of social interaction is the difficulty which participants have in communicating meaningfully about their experience after it is over. They often succeed only in making the program sound highly mysterious and esoteric. This is not surprising. The most profound and significant insights into one's own behavior are often distressingly simple. An individual, for example, may seriously interfere with his effectiveness because he talks too much. For reasons which are psychologically complex, he cannot even hear—let alone understand—ordinary feedback on this matter. Nor does he perceive how his "snowing" others under with words not only interferes with their effectiveness, but defeats his own purposes.

If, as might happen, the T Group experience revealed to him what he was doing to others and to himself, he might, as a result, improve his skill in social interaction substantially. However, he would feel silly telling his colleagues on his return that he had learned the consequences of talking too much. If the insight had led to a real understanding of the intricate significance of this behavior in his adjustment, he would be even more at a loss in talking about it.

There is nothing mysterious about this form of education. It is manipulative only in the sense that it is designed to create conditions under which people may—if they desire—improve their understanding of themselves and of others, and their skills of social interaction. It does tend to demonstrate dramatically what a complex and difficult thing it is to learn even basically simple things in this field. Thus, in describing it, the participant may not communicate very well. That its consequences are of genuine significance, however, is being demonstrated by the growing demand for opportunities to obtain this education.

Incidentally, the criticisms that these programs are examples of "group-think," that they create subservience and conformity to social pressures, undermine individualism, and stifle creativity are based on complete ignorance of the educational methods involved. Almost anyone who has participated in an NTL activity will offer evidence to the contrary. One learns how powerful group pressure can be, but one learns simultaneously how valuable the resources of a group may be in achieving one's own goals. Moreover, one learns something about counteracting the former and utilizing the latter characteristics of group behavior.

As is the case with psychotherapy, these methods of laboratory training in the skills of social interaction will be elaborated and improved greatly in the years ahead. However, they have amply demonstrated their value already.

In Summary

Managerial competence is created on the job, not in the classroom. However, classroom education can be used as a powerful aid to the process of management development, providing there is sufficient understanding of the different kinds of learning which are involved and of the different methods and strategies that are appropriate to these. Only disillusionment can result from the naïve attitude that education is a Good Thing regardless of the need to be met. A few general conclusions seem worthy of reiteration:

1. Classroom learning is effective only within an organizational climate conducive to growth. A negative environment will wipe out the gains from classroom education in a relatively short time.
2. The motivations of the individual—his "felt needs" for new knowledge or increased skill—are absolutely critical factors in any learning. The principle of integration is, therefore, important in the administration of all activities relating to managerial education.
3. Learning is an active process. The "grease gun" conception of education is useless.
4. Practice (experience) and effective feedback are essential aspects of any learning which involves behavior change. Where skills are involved, educational methods which fail to provide for these requirements are valueless.
5. The skills of social interaction are, at the same time, among the most essential for the manager and the most difficult to improve in the classroom. Ordinary methods

of education appear to be relatively ineffective in producing learning in this area. However, laboratory methods providing special conditions for experience and feedback have demonstrated their value.

6. In view of the complexities and difficulties involved in improving managerial competence through classroom learning, our expectations should be modest. This is not to undervalue the contributions of classroom education, but to suggest that managers (like parents vis-à-vis the public school system) sometimes expect formal education to relieve them of responsibility for the growth *on the job* of their subordinates. Attempts to evaluate classroom training programs which ignore the effects of the job climate will inevitably yield misleading results.

REFERENCES

Andrews, Kenneth R., "Is Management Training Effective?" *Harvard Business Review*, vol. 35, nos. 1 and 2 (January–February and March–April), 1957.

Hoy, George A., Jr., "A Brand-new Breakthrough in Management Development," *Factory*, July, 1959.

Johnson, Howard W., "A Framework for Reviewing the Contribution of University Executive Development Programs," Cambridge: Massachusetts Institute of Technology, School of Industrial Management Reprint 27, 1956.

Maier, Norman R. F., Alden R. Solem, and Ayesha A. Maier, *Supervisory and Executive Development: A Manual for Role Playing*. New York: John Wiley & Sons, Inc., 1957.

National Industrial Conference Board, Inc., "Company Programs in Executive Development," Studies in Personnel Policy, no. 107, 1950.

16

The Managerial Team

A few years ago, two of MITs Sloan Fellows undertook a joint master's thesis on the subject of staff-line relationships. One of them concentrated on the accounting function, the other on personnel. They studied several companies and found the usual kinds of difficulties and frictions. The quality of the relationships appeared to have little correlation with the degree of conformity to textbook principles such as unity of command and equality of responsibility and authority.

One division of a large company provided a puzzle. The managers in this organization—line and staff alike—completely ignored the usual distinction between the two types of functions. The researchers found staff people exercising authority quite directly and line people giving advice. *Yet they found little evidence of friction or antagonism between the two groups.* Moreover, the division was regarded as one of the best managed and most economically successful in the company.

The one clue which helped to explain this anomalous situation was the relationship between the general manager and the several managers of both line and staff functions who reported to him. He had been in his job for about two years, and he had created a remarkable spirit of teamwork within this group. They worked together a great deal, and they demonstrated both a high commitment to the objectives they had jointly evolved and a high degree of informal collaboration in achieving them. The formal boundaries between their responsibilities seemed of little consequence to them. Their interest was in getting a job done by whatever means seemed to make sense. The rest of the divisional organization reflected their attitudes.

The conclusion of the researchers was that this group was characterized by a genuine "unity of purpose" which largely obviated the necessity for such formal arrangements as unity of command, equality of authority and responsibility, and staff-line distinctions.

The significance of unity of purpose within a managerial team is given some lip service by most managers, but it is not always recognized that this objective can only be achieved by a closely knit *group.* Most so-called managerial teams are not teams at all, but collections of individual relationships with the boss in which each individual is vying with every other for power, prestige, recognition, and personal autonomy. Under such conditions unity of purpose is a myth.

One research study of top management groups found that 85 per cent of the communications within the group took place between individual subordinates and the superior (up *and* down), and only 15 per cent laterally between the subordinates. Many executives who talk about their "teams" of subordinates would be appalled to discover how low is the actual level of collaboration among them, and how high is the mutual suspicion and antagonism.

Yet these same executives generally create the very conditions which would appall them if recognized. They do so by managing individuals rather than helping to create a genuine group.

The Individual or the Group?

The subject of groups within management tends to generate a good deal of feeling. There are those who have no use for group effort at all and who appear to believe that an organization can operate effectively on the basis of relationships between pairs of individuals. In many companies, for example, committees are held in low esteem. The definition of a camel as a horse put together by a committee reflects a common attitude.

William H. Whyte of *Fortune* magazine, in his *Organization Man,* takes an even stronger position. He argues that group activity has a downward leveling effect on the individual, forces conformity and denies the expression of individualism, nullifies creative activity, and is in general a hampering and limiting form of human activity.

These views deny the realities of organizational life. Many activities simply cannot be carried on and many problems cannot be solved on an individual basis or in two-person relationships. The problem of the group versus the individual is not an either-or problem at all. There are kinds of activities which are appropriate to the individual, others that are appropriate to the pair, and others that are appropriate to larger groups. Under the right conditions, there are positive advantages to be achieved from group effort. In addition, there are severe negative consequences when we ignore the necessity for group action and attempt to solve certain problems in terms of pair relationships.

In general we are remarkably inept in accomplishing objectives through group effort. This is not inevitable. It is a result of inadequate understanding and skill with respect to the unique aspects of group operation. We accept the fact that we have to learn how to operate successfully in our individual relationships with subordinates. If we gave no more time and attention to this phase of managerial activity than we do to group operations, we would experience the same low level of effectiveness in both.

Whyte's thesis that we have given undue emphasis to group phenomena, and in the process lost track of individuals, misses the point altogether. The real problem is that we have given so little attention to group behavior that management does not know enough about how to create the conditions for individual growth and integrity in the group situation. The problem is one of ignorance based on under-, not overemphasis.

Research on group behavior was relatively slow in getting started. For many years, almost the only question that interested psychologists in this field was whether more work got done when people operated together or separately. The tasks selected for study —for example, the performance of mathematical computations— were often not group tasks at all. The researchers failed to differentiate between activities appropriate to the individual and activities appropriate to the group. As a result, the research findings led nowhere.

During the last couple of decades, there has been a concentrated effort to carry on productive research on group behavior, and it is beginning to pay off handsomely. Kurt Lewin and his students initiated this work in the 1930s by asking themselves some meaningful scientific questions: What behavior occurs in face-to-face task-oriented groups, and how does this behavior differ (if it does) from behavior in other situations? Are there variables of forces operating in the group situations which are unique to it? If there are, what are their consequences?

From these beginnings, there has emerged a major field of research endeavor that has produced an impressive body of knowledge. Lewin called this field "group dynamics" because he recognized what has subsequently been verified—that there are important aspects of group behavior which can be best understood by study of the group as a field of forces. He saw this subject as analogous to the physicist's "dynamics."

It often happens that a new field of study, as it turns up findings which challenge long-established and emotionally based convictions, encounters considerable hostility. The intensity of feeling generated by Darwin's study of evolution has died down today, and we regard this field as a legitimate and scientifically respectable one. It is somewhat difficult for the younger generation to appreciate the intensity of feeling that was generated a half century ago over the issues which Darwin raised. Some of us, however, remember the Scopes trial in Tennessee which literally filled the newspapers for some time. Freud's psychoanalysis generated hostilities which have not completely disappeared even today. The field of group dynamics has encountered similar difficulties.

It was natural, as the earlier researchers discovered that there were characteristics of group effort which differentiated this form of human activity from others, to apply their growing insights to practical situations. They began to ask what people could do to be more effective in groups. As this field of application grew, there were of course those who oversold it, and there were others who jumped on the bandwagon to exploit the findings for their own economic ends. Finally, there were the strong feelings of those who feared that emphasis on group behavior would undermine their power. Group dynamics acquired a bad name.

Effective and Ineffective Groups

If we take a balanced and reasonably objective view of the large body of research evidence on group behavior, certain things are clear. First, there are no mysterious and secret skills which will enable the "expert" to manipulate groups toward his own ends. Knowledge in this field, like knowledge in any scientific field, can be misused, but the dangers of its misuse are substantially less than, for example, in the field of atomic physics. In fact, one of the major contributions of research on group behavior has been to show how such manipulative misuse tends to be self-defeating.

Second, despite the rantings of a few "converts," the field is not a cult. It has its own jargon, but consider in comparison the vocabulary that has grown up within the missile field in the past decade!

Third, groups can be effective decision-making and problem-solving entities. All the arguments to the effect that "only the individual" can be responsible, make decisions, innovate, are shibboleths. The fact that many, or even most, groups do not do these things well proves nothing but our lack of knowledge about group behavior and our lack of skill in operating within groups.

The basic questions which the serious researchers in this field are pursuing quite independently of the lunatic fringe are: What forces are uniquely operative in the face-to-face group situations? How do they operate and how can knowledge of them be applied to improve the functioning of groups? This is a worth-while endeavor.

Let us attempt to lay aside for a moment our prejudice, pro or con, with respect to group activity and consider in everyday common-sense terms some of the things that are characteristic of a well-functioning, efficient group. Occasionally, one does encounter a really good top management team or series of staff meetings or committee. What distinguishes such groups from other less effective ones?

1. The "atmosphere," which can be sensed in a few minutes of observation, tends to be informal, comfortable, relaxed. There are no obvious tensions. It is a working atmosphere in which people are involved and interested. There are no signs of boredom.

2. There is a lot of discussion in which virtually everyone participates, but it remains pertinent to the task of the group. If the discussion gets off the subject, someone will bring it back in short order.

3. The task or the objective of the group is well understood and accepted by the members. There will have been free discussion of the objective at some point until it was formulated in such a way that the members of the group could commit themselves to it.

4. The members listen to each other! The discussion does not have the quality of jumping from one idea to another unrelated one. Every idea is given a hearing. People do not appear to be afraid of being foolish by putting forth a creative thought even if it seems fairly extreme.

5. There is disagreement. The group is comfortable with this and shows no signs of having to avoid conflict or to keep everything on a plane of sweetness and light. Disagreements are not suppressed or overridden by premature group action. The reasons are carefully examined, and the group seeks to resolve them rather than to dominate the dissenter.

   On the other hand, there is no "tyranny of the minority." Individuals who disagree do not appear to be trying to dominate the group or to express hostility. Their disagreement is an expression of a genuine difference of opinion, and they expect a hearing in order that a solution may be found.

   Sometimes there are basic disagreements which cannot be resolved. The group finds it possible to live with them, accepting them but not permitting them to block its efforts. Under some conditions, action will be deferred to permit further study of an issue between the members. On other occasions, where the disagreement cannot be resolved and action is necessary, it will be taken but with open caution and recognition that the action may be subject to later reconsideration.

6. Most decisions are reached by a kind of consensus in which it is clear that everybody is in general agreement

and willing to go along. However, there is little tendency for individuals who oppose the action to keep their opposition private and thus let an apparent consensus mask real disagreement. Formal voting is at a minimum; the group does not accept a simple majority as a proper basis for action.

7. Criticism is frequent, frank, and relatively comfortable. There is little evidence of personal attack, either openly or in a hidden fashion. The criticism has a constructive flavor in that it is oriented toward removing an obstacle that faces the group and prevents it from getting the job done.

8. People are free in expressing their feelings as well as their ideas both on the problem and on the group's operation. There is little pussyfooting, there are few "hidden agendas." Everybody appears to know quite well how everybody else feels about any matter under discussion.

9. When action is taken, clear assignments are made and accepted.

10. The chairman of the group does not dominate it, nor on the contrary, does the group defer unduly to him. In fact, as one observes the activity, it is clear that the leadership shifts from time to time, depending on the circumstances. Different members, because of their knowledge or experience, are in a position at various times to act as "resources" for the group. The members utilize them in this fashion and they occupy leadership roles while they are thus being used.

There is little evidence of a struggle for power as the group operates. The issue is not who controls but how to get the job done.

11. The group is self-conscious about its own operations. Frequently, it will stop to examine how well it is doing or what may be interfering with its operation. The prob-

lem may be a matter of procedure, or it may be an individual whose behavior is interfering with the accomplishment of the group's objectives. Whatever it is, it gets open discussion until a solution is found.

These and other observable characteristics are generally found in the effective task group. Every one of them represents important ways of dealing with forces which are present in every group. A substantial amount of sensitivity, understanding, and skill is required of all the members—not of the leader alone—to create such a setting as this.

It has been my privilege to be a member of a staff of six or eight individuals comprising the faculty of an NTL-sponsored training program on a number of occasions. Each time I am impressed anew by the demonstration of effective group action given by these colleagues as they come together to design the program.

Normally a day is set aside for the purpose. The task is clear, but there is always the expectation that this program will contain innovations—perhaps major ones—which will make it not merely different, but better than anything that has been done before. No one knows what these will be, or how they will evolve, but the group confidently expects to use the resources of its members to do a genuinely creative job. This confidence is rarely mistaken.

In addition to designing the program there are dozens of decisions to be made, many necessary assignments of specific tasks and responsibilities, a variety of individual interests and desires to be integrated with the requirements of the program. Conflicts arise and are argued out, sometimes with a lot of heat. These colleagues are individualists, and no one of them is prepared to have his individuality submerged. Nevertheless, there is the kind of commitment to the common purpose that yields genuine self-control.

The task is accomplished with amazing efficiency, yet there is plenty of kidding and good humor. Group "maintenance functions" are performed as the need arises. There is a chairman, but the leadership moves around the group as the situation dictates. Everyone participates actively, yet no one dominates the group. I have never known a vote to be taken except as a joke. Every decision is unanimous.

And, most significant of all, each such group has a different composition. Some individuals may have worked together before, but there are always several new members. Within minutes of the start of the meeting they are as much a part of the group as if they had been members for years.

It is truly an exhilarating experience to participate in such an activity. I usually come away wishing some of my good friends in management who have a jaundiced view of groups could have observed the meeting.

Now let us look at the other end of the range. Consider a poor group—one that is relatively ineffective in accomplishing its purposes. What are some of the observable characteristics of its operation?

1. The "atmosphere" is likely to reflect either indifference and boredom (people whispering to each other or carrying on side conversations, individuals who are obviously not involved, etc.) or tension (undercurrents of hostility and antagonism, stiffness and undue formality, etc.). The group is clearly not challenged by its task or genuinely involved in it.

2. A few people tend to dominate the discussion. Often their contributions are way off the point. Little is done by anyone to keep the group clearly on the track.

3. From the things which are said, it is difficult to understand what the group task is or what its objectives are. These may have been stated by the chairman initially,

but there is no evidence that the group either understands or accepts a common objective. On the contrary, it is usually evident that different people have different, private, and personal objectives which they are attempting to achieve in the group, and that these are often in conflict with each other and with the group's task.

4. People do not really listen to each other. Ideas are ignored and overridden. The discussion jumps around with little coherence and no sense of movement along a track. One gets the impression that there is much talking for effect—people make speeches which are obviously intended to impress someone else rather than being relevant to the task at hand.

   Conversation with members after the meeting will reveal that they have failed to express ideas or feelings which they may have had for fear they would be criticized or regarded as silly. Some members feel that the leader or the other members are constantly making judgments of them in terms of evaluations of the contributions they make, and so they are extremely careful about what they say.

5. Disagreements are generally not dealt with effectively by the group. They may be completely suppressed by a leader who fears conflict. On the other hand, they may result in open warfare, the consequences of which is domination by one subgroup over another. They may be "resolved" by a vote in which a very small majority wins the day, and a large minority remains completely unconvinced.

   There may be a "tyranny of the minority" in which an individual or a small subgroup is so aggressive that the majority accedes to their wishes in order to preserve the peace or to get on with the task. In general only the more aggressive members get their ideas considered because the less aggressive people tend either to keep quiet altogether or to give up after short, ineffectual attempts to be heard.

6. Actions are often taken prematurely before the real issues are either examined or resolved. There will be much grousing after the meeting by people who disliked the decision but failed to speak up about it in the meeting itself. A simple majority is considered sufficient for action, and the minority is expected to go along. Most of the time, however, the minority remains resentful and uncommitted to the decision.

7. Action decisions tend to be unclear—no one really knows who is going to do what. Even when assignments of responsibility are made, there is often considerable doubt as to whether they will be carried out.

8. The leadership remains clearly with the committee chairman. He may be weak or strong, but he sits always "at the head of the table."

9. Criticism may be present, but it is embarrassing and tension-producing. It often appears to involve personal hostility, and the members are uncomfortable with this and unable to cope with it. Criticism of ideas tends to be destructive. Sometimes every idea proposed will be "clobbered" by someone else. Then, no one is willing to stick his neck out.

10. Personal feelings are hidden rather than being out in the open. The general attitude of the group is that these are inappropriate for discussion and would be too explosive if brought out on the table.

11. The group tends to avoid any discussion of its own "maintenance." There is often much discussion after the meeting of what was wrong and why, but these matters are seldom brought up and considered within the meeting itself where they might be resolved.

Why is it that so many groups seem to resemble this example rather than the first one? There are a number of reasons. In the first place, most of us have rather low expectations of group accomplishment. Our experience with really effective groups has been so limited that we do not have clear standards of what could be. In the second place, most of us have relatively little knowledge of what is important to good group functioning. We are not aware of current research findings concerning the significant requirements for effective group operations, and therefore the things we attempt to do to improve a given group are not always relevant.

One of the most important reasons for poor group functioning is the general fear of conflict and hostility which leads us to behave in ways that hamper rather than help. Hostilities, hidden agendas, and other personal factors inimical to group functioning are very commonly present, particularly with a newly constituted group. To ignore these or to suppress them is to let them determine the level of effectiveness of the group. Yet, our fear of personal feuding and conflict is such that that is exactly what normally happens.

Another significant factor resulting in poor group activity is the mistaken idea that the effectiveness of the group depends solely upon the leader. As a matter of fact, the research evidence indicates quite clearly that *skillful and sensitive membership behavior is the real clue to effective group operation.* In a really competent and skilled group, the members can in fact carry on a highly effective operation with no designated leader whatever.

Finally, along with our fears of conflict and hostility, is a lack of recognition of the necessity for paying attention to the maintenance of the group itself. Like any complex organization, a group requires attention to its functioning. If it is to operate at peak efficiency, it will require constant maintenance. Most groups deal with maintenance problems only in the post mortems outside the meetings, and these seldom result in action within the group.

Behind all these specifics, frequently, is a deeper attitude associated with Theory X: Management by direction and control is jeopardized by effective group functioning. The principle of "divide and rule" is eminently sound if one wishes to exercise personal power over subordinates. It is the best way to control them.

If, however, the superior recognizes the existence of the intricate interdependence characteristic of modern industry, and if he is less interested in personal power than in creating conditions such that the human resources available to him will be utilized to achieve organizational purposes, he will seek to build a strong group. He will recognize that the highest commitment to organizational objectives, and the most successful collaboration in achieving them, *require unique kinds of interaction which can only occur in a highly effective group setting.* He will in fact discourage discussion or decision making on many matters which affect his organization except in the group setting. He will give the idea of "the team" full expression, with all the connotations it carries on the football field.

The Potentialities of Teamwork

The face-to-face group is as significant a unit of organization as the individual. The two are not antithetical. In a genuinely effective group the individual finds some of his deepest satisfactions. Through teamwork and group activity many of the difficult organizational problems of coordination and control can be solved. However, these values can be realized only if certain requirements are met.

First, we will have to abandon the idea that individual and group values are necessarily opposed, that the latter can only be realized at the expense of the former. If we would look to the family, we might recognize the possibilities inherent in the opposite point of view.

Second, we will have to give serious attention to the matter of acquiring understanding of the factors which determine the effectiveness of group action and to the acquisition of skill in utilizing them. This means much more than offering courses in conference leadership. It means, above all, acquiring skills in group *membership*. The laboratory method of training developed by the National Training Laboratory (discussed in Chapter 15) is a particularly effective one for acquiring these skills.

Third, we will need to learn to distinguish between those activities which are appropriate for groups and those that are not.

Finally, we will need to distinguish between the team concept of management as a gimmick to be applied within the strategy of management by direction and control and the team concept as a natural correlate of management by integration and self-control. The one has nothing in common with the other.

To the extent that these requirements are met, we will make some significant discoveries. For example:

1. Group target setting offers advantages that cannot be achieved by individual target setting alone. The two are supplementary, not mutually exclusive.
2. An effective managerial group provides the best possible environment for individual development. It is the natural place to broaden the manager's understanding of functions other than his own and to create a genuine appreciation of the need for collaboration. It is the best possible training ground for skill in problem solving and in social interaction.
3. Many significant objectives and measures of performance can be developed for the group which cannot be applied to the individual. The members of cohesive groups will work at least as hard to achieve group objectives as they will to achieve individual ones.
4. In an effective managerial team the aspects of "dog-eat-dog" competition, which are actually inimical to organizational accomplishment, can be minimized by the develop-

ment of "unity of purpose" without reducing individual motivation.

It seems to me unlikely that the transition will be rapid from our conception of an organization as a pattern of individual relationships to one of a pattern of relationships among groups. We have too much to learn, and too many prejudices to overcome. I do believe, however, that such a transition is inevitable in the long run. We cannot hope much longer to operate the complex, interdependent, collaborative enterprise which is the modern industrial company on the completely unrealistic premise that it consists of individual relationships. The costs of doing so—although they are mostly hidden and unrecognized—are completely unjustifiable. When a few managements begin to discover the economic as well as the psychological advantages of really effective team operation, their competitive advantage will provide all the stimulus necessary to accelerate this transition.

Fads will come and go. The fundamental fact of man's capacity to collaborate with his fellows in the face-to-face group will survive the fads and one day be recognized. Then, and only then, will management discover how seriously it has underestimated the true potential of its human resources.

REFERENCES

Bennis, Warren G., and Herbert A. Shepard, "A Theory of Group Development," *Human Relations,* vol. 9, 1956.

Cartwright, Dorwin, and Alvin Zander, *Group Dynamics, Research and Theory.* Evanston, Ill.: Row, Peterson & Company, 1953.

Coser, Lewis A., "The Functions of Small Group Research," *Social Problems,* vol. 3, no. 1, 1955.

Fiedler, Fred E., *Leader Attitudes and Group Effectiveness.* Urbana, Ill.: University of Illinois Press, 1958.

Gordon, Thomas, *Group Centered Leadership.* Boston: Houghton Mifflin Company, 1955.

Hare, A. Paul, Edgar F. Borgatta, and Robert F. Bales, *Small Groups.* New York: Alfred A. Knopf, Inc., 1955.

National Training Laboratory in Group Development, *Explorations in Human Relations Training: An Assessment of Experience, 1947–1953*. Washington, D.C.: 1953.

Olmsted, Michael S., *The Small Group*. New York: Random House, Inc., 1959. (Paperback SS 16.)

Thelen, Herbert, *Dynamics of Groups at Work*. Chicago: University of Chicago Press, 1954.

CONCLUSION

Developments in physical science theory during the first half of the twentieth century have led to the creation of a new world. If anyone had been able to predict in 1900 what life in the United States would be like in 1960, he would have been regarded as a complete fool. Passenger travel 6 to 8 miles above the earth at 600 miles per hour, space vehicles circling the moon, radar, a nuclear-powered submarine traveling under the icecap at the North Pole, air conditioning, television, frozen foods, stereophonic reproduction of the music of world-renowned musicians in the home—these things and hundreds more were almost inconceivable sixty years ago. They would still be inconceivable were it not for developments in scientific theory and man's inventive genius in exploiting them.

Although the parallel may seem unreasonable to some, we are today in a period when the development of theory within the social sciences will permit innovations which are at present inconceivable. Among these will be dramatic changes in the organization and management of economic enterprise. The capacities of the average human being for creativity, for growth, for collaboration, for productivity (in the full sense of the term) are far greater than we yet have recognized. If we don't destroy life on this planet before we discover how to make it possible for man to utilize his abilities to create a world in which he can live in peace, it is possible that the next half century will bring the most dramatic social changes in human history.

1 believe that the industrial enterprise is a microcosm within which some of the most basic of these social changes will be invented and tested and refined. As Peter Drucker has pointed out, the modern, large, industrial enterprise is itself a social invention of great historical importance. Unfortunately, it is already obsolete. In its present form it is simply not an adequate means for meeting the future economic requirements of society. The fundamental difficulty is that we have not yet learned enough about organizing and managing the human resources of enterprise. Fortunately, an increasing number of managers recognize the inadequacy of present methods. In this recognition lies the hope of the future. Industrial management has again and again demonstrated an amazing ability to innovate once it is persuaded of the opportunity to do so.

Management is severely hampered today in its attempts to innovate with respect to the human side of enterprise by the inadequacy of conventional organization theory. Based on invalid and limiting assumptions about human behavior, this theory blinds us to many possibilities for invention, just as the physical science theory of a half century ago prevented even the perception of the possibility of radar or space travel.

It is not important that management accept the assumptions of Theory Y. These are one man's interpretations of current social science knowledge, and they will be modified—possibly supplanted —by new knowledge within a short time. It *is* important that management abandon limiting assumptions like those of Theory X, so that future inventions with respect to the human side of enterprise will be more than minor changes in already obsolescent conceptions of organized human effort.

Theoretical assumptions such as those of Theory Y imply some conditions which are unrealizable in practice (like the perfect vacuum implied by physical theory). This is not a handicap; it is the stimulus to invention and discovery. Assumptions like those of Theory X provide us with no standard except present accomplishment and thus encourage us, as Joe Scanlon was fond of saying, to "face the past and back into the future."

The ideas with respect to changed managerial strategies consistent with Theory Y which have been discussed in this volume—target setting, the Scanlon Plan, participation, the professional role of staff, the "agricultural" approach to management development—are no more than beginning steps toward management by integration and self-control. Once management becomes truly persuaded that it is seriously underestimating the potential represented by its human resources—once it accepts assumptions about human behavior more consistent with current social science knowledge than those of Theory X—it will invest the time, money, and effort not only to develop improved applications of such ideas as have been discussed in these pages, but to invent more effective ones. As always, however, invention will go hand in hand with new theory.

The purpose of this volume is not to entice management to choose sides over Theory X or Theory Y. It is, rather, to encourage the realization that theory is important, to urge management to examine its assumptions and make them explicit. In doing so it will open a door to the future. The possible result could be developments during the next few decades with respect to the human side of enterprise comparable to those that have occurred in technology during the past half century.

And, if we can learn how to realize the potential for collaboration inherent in the human resources of industry, we will provide a model for governments and nations which mankind sorely needs.